SIR ROGER

THE LIFE AND TIMES OF ROGER HUNT,
A Liverpool Legend

by Ivan Ponting & Steve Hale

ACKNOWLEDGEMENTS

The author would like to thank photographer Steve Hale, Ian Callaghan, Bobby Charlton, Tommy Smith, Phil Thompson, Steve Small, Eddie Marks, Tony Williams, Les Gold, Colin Wilkinson, Pat, Rosie and Joe Ponting, the Barretts of Great Crosby and, of course, Roger Hunt himself.

Published by:
The Bluecoat Press
Bluecoat Chambers
Liverpool L1 3BX

Design: Steve Small

Origination: Typebase Limited, Liverpool

Print: Stanley Printing Company, Liverpool

ISBN 1 872568 27 0

INTRODUCTION

With the exception of Bill Shankly himself, Roger Hunt was the most potent and enduring symbol of the epoch-making Liverpool side of the 1960s.

The modest Lancastrian was a lovely, uplifting footballer - arguably the most underrated of his generation, and that despite his noble contribution to England's World Cup triumph of 1966 - yet his true eminence, the unique niche he occupies in Merseyside folklore, stems from far more than mere playing considerations.

Hunt's goal-scoring feats as the Reds embarked on a quarter of a century's unprecedented near-dominance of the English game are enshrined, with due reverence, in the record books. But the bare statistics, mightily impressive though they are, can't begin to measure the impact of the man on the city's contemporary scene.

It is tempting, at the outset of this tale, to give pride of place to testimony from the host of soccer alumni who have queued, down the years, to pay glittering tribute to Hunt - the likes of Sir Alf Ramsey, the late Bobby Moore or the aforementioned Shanks, for example.

Then there is Bobby Charlton, who during the preparation of this book engineered time in his horrendously busy schedule to speak affectionately and at length about his former international team-mate. Sir Bobby was characteristically and touchingly eager to share with Roger the credit for some of his own most famous achievements, but more of that in due course.

Equally, the recollections of his Anfield comrades-in-arms, such men as Ian Callaghan, Tommy Smith and Ron Yeats, who perhaps know him better than anyone, will unfold on the pages that follow.

But first, it seems more appropriate to consider the impressions of a witness who watched the Hunt career unfold from that most emotional and relevant of vantage points, the Kop.

For the best part of three decades, beginning in the 1950s, only virulent illness would keep Stan Green from his spot on that most revered of terraces. From there he monitored in minute detail the early development, the glorious pomp and what he saw as the premature departure of Roger Hunt.

A perceptive, articulate fellow, now a consultant flooring contractor in Childwall and seemingly not a man given to flights of nostalgic fancy, Stan nevertheless comes over slightly misty-eyed as he conjures up a mind's-eye image of his boyhood hero.

'He was special, not just for what he did, but for what he was. The rest of that wonderful team Bill Shankly put together in the early '60s were idols, every last man of them, but Roger was also the guy next door, an everyday sort of chap. Watching him, you felt he was a mate, everybody's mate. Somehow he was not only playing for Liverpool, but also for the folks in the ground who were kicking every ball with him.

'Roger Hunt had the common touch and he fed people's dreams. They liked to think if Roger could do it, then so could they. It was almost as if the Reds had been a man short so Shanks had pulled Roger out of the Kop and he'd started playing.

'To me, he was the heart of Liverpool FC, a magnificent footballer yet so unassuming and quiet with it. He symbolised all that was good about the club. There are degrees of worship for such men as Keegan and Rush and Dalglish. But Hunt was different. People didn't just marvel at what he could do, they loved him.'

Indeed, so crucial a component of Shanks' first great team was Roger that many fans could not believe it when he was allowed to leave for Bolton Wanderers just before Christmas 1969.

Stan Green again: 'To me, and thousands like me, Roger Hunt was like John Wayne. He seemed indestructible. Somehow, in my mind he could be playing now. The decision to let him go was stunning. I felt he had been cast into a leper colony - with all due respects to Bolton! - for no reason at all'

As he finished the sentence, Stan grinned, acknowledging the part youthful hero-worship played in his sentiment but emphasising that, even so, it was real enough.

'Shanks used to say that the fans deserved so much. They queued for hours to part with their hard-earned cash so they could travel all over the land to watch Liverpool. Therefore he reckoned that if any player didn't give his absolute all for the cause then he should be locked up. But even if Bill had power to make good his threat - and I would put nothing past that man! - we all knew that Roger would never be put away.

'No matter how badly things might be going on the pitch, his head never went down. There was no way he was ever going to short-change the supporters. Sure, like anyone else, he might miss a sitter, but you could bet your life he'd worked his butt off to get into a scoring position in the first place. He gave the impression that he would have died to score for Liverpool, provided it was within the rules.

'That was the other thing about Roger. Though he was brave and would give and take in fair conflict, he would never do anything underhand. No matter how hard he had sprinted to reach a ball, he would pull out rather than risk kicking the 'keeper. He was a total gent.

'And what a player! In those days it used to be possible to swap ends of the ground at half-time and I used to do that so I could be behind the goal Roger was attacking. He had fantastic mobility, more skill than most people gave him credit for and he would shoot from almost any angle or distance. No matter what the circumstances of any given game, he was always liable to pop the ball in the net.

'All in all he was . . .' *(Stan paused to find the right words)* '. . . a jewel, utterly priceless.'

Throughout numerous happy weeks spent on Merseyside researching this volume, I found Stan Green's fervent and sincere regard for the Liverpool and England marksman wholly typical. In the course of countless conversations I heard not one syllable of criticism uttered against Roger Hunt, and that despite raking through the memories of hardened professionals who were quite capable of dispensing vitriol in respect of other household names.

On a personal level, I spent many hours with the man who has scored more League goals for Liverpool than anyone else, finding him amiable, generous and delightfully down-to-earth.

He continues to greet the bouquets which engulf him on Merseyside with the same matter-of-fact realism with which he met the brickbats of carping, mostly southern-based critics throughout his England career. There could be no more wholesome or inspiring example to young lads on the threshold of a career in the game.

No wonder they call him Sir Roger . . .

Ivan Ponting, October 1995.

A PRETTY SOUND DECISION . . .

Like so many footballers of his generation, Roger Hunt owed a huge debt to a tennis ball. Growing up in the homely little village of Culcheth, which nestles comfortably just off the busy East Lancs Road linking Liverpool to Manchester, he carried that ball with him everywhere. At every opportunity, he would fish it out of his pocket and kick it against walls, kerbstones, fences - anything that would send it bouncing back to his eager feet.

In later years, as he starred in two League title-winning campaigns and an FA Cup Final victory for Liverpool and played an inestimably important role as his country lifted the World Cup, he had cause to give thanks for that childhood obsession.

Soccer pundits tended not to dwell on his ball skill, yet while it was not present to the droolworthy degree of, say, George Best's or Peter Thompson's, it was not a common occurrence for him to lose possession through poor control.

Liverpool always placed great emphasis on obtaining total mastery of the ball - it was one of Shankly's golden tenets in training - yet Roger maintains that the basis of his prowess was laid on the way to and from Leigh Grammar School.

'I learned techniques as a boy that stood me in good stead for my whole career. Sadly, it's not safe for kids to play with a ball in the streets nowadays, and there are so many more leisure attractions competing for their time. That's why the overall level of skill in football has decreased,' he reckons.

Roger's infatuation with the game dates as far back as he can remember, to the days before the Hunt family moved the four miles to Culcheth from Glazebury, the village of his birth, in 1944 when he was six years old.

He and his younger brother, Peter, saw little of their father, who had launched a haulage business: 'My dad and my uncle started with a lorry apiece and they worked fantastically hard to make it grow into a successful concern. Occasionally I would go out in the lorry but it was all forms of sport, football in particular, which dominated my life.

However, this is not the tale of a boy-wonder who always knew he was destined for stardom. Though consumed by the ambition to be a professional, playing for his school team on Saturday mornings and for a local side in the afternoons, there was little early inkling that he would make the grade. His enthusiasm was limitless and he was obviously an extremely useful goal-scoring inside-forward for his age, but that extra-special something which lifts the extravagantly gifted lad beyond the reach of his peers was not in evidence.

Roger persisted, though, and when he was 16 he signed for Stockton Heath (later to become Warrington Town) and found himself lining up alongside men in the competitive, combative mid-Cheshire League.

His opponents played their football for fun but they took it deadly seriously, and were not disposed to make allowances for the blond newcomer's tender years. Had his determination wavered one iota, his dream might have died there and then; but, in fact, he prospered, standing out and netting prolifically at the higher level.

Indeed, so promisingly did Roger perform that his manager, Freddie Worrall - who had helped Portsmouth shock Wolves to lift the FA Cup in 1939 - recommended him to the south coast club.

Roger recalls: 'There was real talk of me going to Fratton Park, but nothing materialised. By now I was 17 and had left school to start work for my dad. I passed my driving test and a future in the haulage business seemed to be mapped out for me. But every mile I drove that lorry I was still burning inside to be a footballer and I decided to write off to League clubs, asking for trials, hoping to strike lucky.'

His personal favourites had always been Bolton Wanderers, then (in the mid 1950s) a

Opposite: Man at the wheel. Roger looks at home in the cab of one of the family lorries, but his career was to take him in another direction.

9

Playing the Army game: Roger (standing, fourth from the right) lines up with his Royal Artillery team-mates at Larkhill on Salisbury Plain.

major force in the First Division, and the young man would have given anything to have become a team-mate of his idol, Nat Lofthouse (ironically, Nat would one day recruit Roger to the Burnden Park cause).

But his typically level-headed reasoning was that competition for places would be less fiery in slightly less exalted surroundings, so he dashed off his first missive to Second Division Bury.

Accordingly he was invited to Gigg Lane to show what he could do and made a favourable enough impression for the Shakers to sign him on amateur forms. Dave Russell, later to manage Tranmere Rovers, was the boss, but Roger came mainly under the aegis of Bert Head, who ran the reserves and was an immensely shrewd judge of a player.

Bert clearly rated his raw recruit highly, but being in and out of the Gigg Lane 'B' team didn't satisfy the youngster, who was training twice a week with Bury and had no car. He lived a two-hour bus journey away in Culcheth, and before long fitting eight hours of public transport around his working commitments each week began to lose its appeal.

'I didn't seem to be making much progress so I screwed up my nerve and put my feelings to Bert Head. I told him I was desperately keen to play pro football but needed to know one way or the other. He asked me to come for a month's full-time training, after which a decision would be made.'

Roger needed no prompting to accept the offer and relished working alongside people who made their living from the game he loved, deriving a particular thrill from training with Stan Pearson, the illustrious former Manchester United and England inside-forward who was then approaching retirement.

'It was a lovely set-up at Bury. In those days even small clubs had more than 30 professionals, and they had a smashing training ground known as Lower Gigg Lane. When my stint was up, Bert Head wanted me but Dave Russell harboured doubts and asked me back for another month. I agreed, but was finally overcome by frustration when I found myself a reserve to the reserves (there were no substitutes in those days) so I was little more than a kitman.

'At that stage I rang Bert and told him I would rather be playing, even if it was at a local level, so I was going back to Stockton Heath. He warned me I was making the mistake of my life, but left it at that.'

Now Roger felt his hopes slipping away: 'I'll be honest, I thought that maybe I wasn't good enough after all and didn't write any more letters, though in retrospect I find that difficult to explain. After all, Bert had seen something in me.'

Back in the Mid-Cheshire League he scored heavily once more, but as he prepared for his National Service in 1957, he was increasingly resigned to playing football for fun and making his living behind the wheel of a truck.

Initially, at least, his spell in the Army did little to alter his pessimistic outlook: 'I had no real pedigree, had not won any schoolboy or youth international caps, so there was no chance of a posting where plenty of football would be guaranteed. So as an ordinary squaddie in the Royal Artillery I found myself at Oswestry and then Rhyl.'

Next came a move to Larkhill on Salisbury Plain, one of the bleakest, most isolated landscapes in England and not a place where he expected to further his waning ambition. But, as Roger was to discover, the game flourishes in even the most far-flung of outposts and his soccer development continued apace in Wiltshire's wide-open spaces.

Though the Army didn't greet him as a feted starlet, the top sporting brass recognised rapidly that they had a high-quality performer on their hands and he was pitched straight into his regimental team.

For the unassuming but fiercely determined youngster, the goals flowed as readily as they had back home, and his reputation began to burgeon. It would be an exaggeration to say that big-time scouts were camping outside his barracks, but one night after a game against the Pay Corps - which boasted an enterprising side including the likes of future Arsenal flankman Alan Skirton and utility forward Bobby Jones, destined to become a Bristol Rovers stalwart - he was approached by two representatives of Devizes Town.

Roger recalls: 'I decided I had nothing to lose by sampling life in the local league and I was glad I did. I enjoyed my spell with Devizes immensely, especially helping them to win the Wiltshire Cup, and I made a lot of good friends. I found myself very busy, what with my Army duties, turning out for the Town and then, one week in three, going back north to play for Stockton Heath.'

Thus Roger was in two shop windows, and there proved to be no shortage of potential

The strip is unfamiliar but the style is unmistakable. Resplendent in the stripes of Devizes Town, Roger nets against Calne in a Wiltshire Cup semi-final.

customers. While cutting a swathe through defences in Cheshire, he gained the notice of Bill Jones, a reliable defender for Liverpool in the immediate post-war years who had become a talent-spotter for the Anfield club.

Bill passed on a glowing recommendation to the Reds' manager, Phil Taylor, and Roger was offered the chance to show his mettle for Liverpool's junior teams.

It seems difficult to imagine now, but in the late 1950s the Merseysiders were no more than a proficient but depressingly unambitious Second Division outfit - how that would be transformed come the Shankly Revolution! - but they represented a golden lifeline to a young man who was not especially enamoured of spending his working life in the cab of a lorry.

This initial acquaintance with the Reds, during leave from the Army, went well, and he continued to sparkle for little Devizes, attracting the attention of an old friend in the process.

By then Bert Head, late of Bury, was occupying the boss's chair at Swindon Town, Wiltshire's only professional club, and when he noted the progress of his erstwhile protege, in whom he had always believed, he was anxious to secure the lad's services at the second time of asking.

Now Roger was to face an agonising dilemma. Having progressed to Liverpool's reserves, for whom he had scored on each outing, he was given the opportunity of full-time professional terms at Anfield.

But Head stepped in with a slightly better cash deal plus a club house, a tempting offer for a 20-year-old who was newly married (to Patricia, a Lancashire lass). True, Third Division Swindon were lower in status than the Reds, but their manager outlined ambitious plans which suggested that would be merely a temporary situation.

Many might have opted for the more appealing financial package, but Roger was - and remains - a home bird at heart. Freddie Worrall, his old mentor at Stockton Heath, confirmed the boy's gut feeling that he should head for Merseyside.

'Freddie reckoned it was worth taking less to be in my own environment. He told me that in his days at Portsmouth, he had often pined for Warrington - some might find that difficult to believe! - and I needed little persuading.'

Thus did Roger Hunt throw in his lot with Liverpool FC, which turned out to be a pretty sound decision . . .

A RED STAR IS BORN

Come August 1959, Roger Hunt found himself in an enviable situation. Twenty-one years old with the world at his feet, he had recently signed a contract with Liverpool; he was on the ladder, admittedly still occupying a lowly rung, which might conceivably, if he worked hard and was lucky, lead to soccer stardom. If he failed to make the grade, either through ill fortune or because he simply wasn't up to the task, he had the reassuring security of a berth in the family business on which to fall back.

Not that Roger had the slightest intention of needing that career safety net. Indeed, nets of a different nature were his priority and before long he would be filling them with gratifying regularity.

Yet rapid though the transition from promising rookie to free-scoring first-team regular proved to be, it was never something he regarded as inevitable and did not come without much critical self-examination and quite fearsome dedication.

Roger recalls: 'I've got to admit that, despite the faith shown in me by people whose judgement I respected, I left the Army with some slight residual fear that I might not be quite good enough. I was confident in my own way, but I suppose my earlier rejection by Bury had sown a tiny seed of doubt.

'I knew perfectly well that I wasn't an out-and-out natural, the sort who can make a ball talk, so it was down to me to compensate for it in other ways. I made up my mind that if I didn't succeed at Anfield then it wouldn't be for the lack of determination. From the first day I threw myself into training, ran and tackled for everything and practised my ball skills at every opportunity.'

The need for such single-minded industry had become clear to Roger during his appearances for the Reds' junior sides while on Army leave. At the time he wasn't as fit as the lads who were in full-time training, and he suffered for it.

Happily, he was under the protective wing of Joe Fagan, then just one of the training staff but later to manage the club with huge success. Roger grins affectionately as he recalls the influence of the shrewd, firm, but essentially avuncular taskmaster:

'There was one game against Preston which we had to win to secure talent money for the reserves. Quickly it became clear that I was struggling to keep up, and at half-time Joe started to say he wanted more from me. But then he saw I was practically on my knees and he would never persecute anyone who was trying their best, so he left it.

'Half-way through the second half I swapped positions with our centre-half John Nicholson (who was destined to die in a road accident in 1966) but we lost 2-1. Afterwards Joe took me to one side. Without being critical, he spelt out exactly what would be needed if I was going to have a chance of making it in football.'

Fagan's blueprint amounted to graft, graft and more graft - and with nothing guaranteed on the end of it.

'I talked this over with my dad on the way home in the car and he said that maybe I should forget about football as a career. But Joe continued to encourage me and was always a huge influence as I went on to reach the first team. I could always confide in him or ask his advice. He was always there and I can never thank him enough.'

Clearly, Roger Hunt was ideal raw material for the Liverpool method of advancement, based on doing the simple things well and paying attention to detail, and those early lessons learned from such men as Fagan were taken to heart.

Thus equipped with an exemplary attitude, he excelled in his first pre-season training as a professional and he made a fruitful start for the reserves, scoring seven times in five games.

It was a fabulous experience for the quiet, still rather wide-eyed youngster to turn out

alongside such men as veteran defenders Geoff Twentyman and Laurie Hughes, former first-team regulars whose careers were now winding down, and there had even been the occasional opportunity to partner Billy Liddell, arguably the greatest player in the club's history, now in his 38th year and slowing down at last.

In his first year as a pro, and in the days when big clubs carried staffs of some 40 footballers, a regular niche in the second team represented highly acceptable progress. But even more dramatic advancement was on the horizon.

The Reds had made a disappointing start to the 1959/60 campaign, losing three of their first five Second Division encounters, and Phil Taylor decided his attack needed a fresh cutting edge. So for the visit to Anfield of Scunthorpe United on Wednesday September the ninth, less than two months after being demobbed from the Army, Roger Hunt was called up for his senior debut.

What made it even more special was that he was to replace no less a personage than Billy Liddell at centre-forward - the great man was nursing a niggling injury - and Roger cherishes vivid memories of that milestone evening in his young life.

'It was a weird sensation running out in front of nearly 32,000 people. The most I had known before was a couple of thousand, and now I was confronted by a sea of expectant faces. It was a huge shock to the system.'

That probably had plenty to do with Roger's uncharacteristically wan first-half performance in which he struggled to adjust to the pace and tenor of the game. He wasn't accustomed to a pattern of play which was considerably more sophisticated than anything he had encountered before, and it showed.

His discomfort came to a head after 23 minutes when he missed an inviting chance to give Liverpool the lead, and he was mightily relieved when Jimmy Melia managed to put the Reds in front two minutes later.

Significantly, though, he never lost heart - how often that observation could be made during the rest of his career - and some 20 minutes into the second period came the sweet moment that wiped away all the anguish that had gone before.

The clever Melia glided a short free-kick to Roger on the edge of the box. Had the new-boy tried to be slick, perhaps attempting an elaborate set-up for one of his converging colleagues, the chance would have been lost. But, glory be, he allowed instinct to take over and just swung his right foot with all his might. The ball boomed past a startled Ken Hardwick between the Scunthorpe posts, cannoned against the crossbar and glanced down to nestle satisfyingly in the corner of the net.

As well as confirming Liverpool's hold on the match, that strike proved a defining moment in the Hunt development. With a goal against his name, his confidence mushroomed; suddenly he seemed to have an extra yard of pace, his demeanour was no longer tentative and he looked threatening every time he received the ball.

When the final whistle sounded he was shattered by the physical exertion of his first League game, but deliriously happy with the outcome. Clearly, he was not the finished article, but equally apparent was that the Anfield coaching staff had custody of an as-yet uncut gem whose ultimate value was incalculable.

That opinion was reflected by the next morning's newspaper headlines which included: 'New boy Hunt cracks in a beauty' and 'Liverpool's new leader a find'. The match reports, too, offered generous praise with the writer for the now-long-defunct *News Chronicle and Daily Dispatch* purring: 'Hunt . . . may not be an orthodox centre-forward, but by lying deep he emphasised his footballing ability, creative artistry and control.'

The *Daily Mail's* Don Mosey referred to Roger's perfectly-judged short passes, neat deflections, lovely body-swerve and cracking right-foot shot, while Alf Ballard of the late, lamented *Daily Herald* summed up with 'when he gained confidence he held the line together well.'

For the record, the Liverpool team that night comprised Doug Rudham in goal, full-backs John Molyneux and Ronnie Moran, half-backs Bobby Campbell, Dick White and Barry Wilkinson and a forward line of Johnny Morrissey, Jimmy Melia, Roger, Jimmy Harrower and Alan A'Court. Most of these would be swept away by the whirlwind that was to descend on

Opposite: Portrait of a rookie. In the early years of Roger's career, posing for photographs was something of a novelty, but as the seasons went by the clicking of cameras would become a constant accompaniment as he went about his business.

Anfield three months later. Indeed, Roger would be the only man to retain his place throughout the triumphant Shankly-inspired decade that was in store.

However, if the portents seemed favourable for the rookie Hunt after his fulfilling debut, there was no danger of either club or player getting carried away. Manager Phil Taylor drew Hunt to one side and told him that he had done well - and then informed him that he would be replaced by Liddell for the home game with Middlesbrough on the Saturday.

Roger looks back: 'I wasn't really surprised. He told me my time would come and, as things turned out, I didn't have to wait long. The lads lost to 'Boro and I was brought back for the return against Scunthorpe the following Thursday, this time at inside-right with Jimmy Harrower making way.

'I did enough in a goalless draw to keep my place for the next game at Derby, where I managed to score the winner. That whole trip had been a huge novelty for me, staying away for the two games and putting up in a hotel in Buxton. Despite my time in the Army I hadn't travelled extensively and this made it seem like I'd really hit the big time!

'After that, for a while, I couldn't seem to put a foot wrong and my self-belief positively surged. The goals continued to come - I remember one 35-yarder in a 4-1 home win over Plymouth - and I seemed to be getting established.'

One of the joys of this period for Roger was occasional outings in the same side as Billy Liddell, who had lost a lot of his power and pace but none of his presence.

'He was the very epitome of what a professional should be. Billy never shouted the odds but was always ready to pass on his experience to the youngsters. He helped me hugely in his quiet, unobtrusive way, giving me advice that stood me in good stead as long as I stayed in football.

'My only regret was that I didn't play alongside him at his best. As I was setting out, he was coming to an end, but still he exerted a massive influence. Still the crowd loved him, and the generation that was lucky enough to watch him in action week after week will always feel that way.'

Roger is far too self-effacing to make the point - perhaps even too modest to realise it - but now, in the mid 1990s, those simple but heartfelt sentiments are equally applicable to himself.

Opposite: Kicking in before a game during 1960/61, Bill Shankly's first full campaign at the Anfield helm. That term Roger contributed 19 goals in 36 senior starts, but much better was to come.

ALL CHANGE AT ANFIELD

Plenty have written about the wind of change that gusted through Anfield with the arrival of Bill Shankly. In fact, it was more like a hurricane and it carried all before it. Indeed, it blew the cobwebs off the cobwebs!

And while it would be inappropriate to re-chronicle the renaissance in exhaustive detail - that would entail converting the title of this book from 'Sir Roger' to 'King Bill' - the tales of Hunt and Liverpool are so inextricably entwined that some exposition is required.

Under a well-meaning but woefully unimaginative board and with the courteous Phil Taylor, an honoured former skipper of the club, at the managerial helm, the Reds were tootling along quite nicely and safely near the top of the Second Division.

But Liverpool FC was riddled with complacency, apparently content to be a second-class member of the soccer community, which was nothing short of an insult to the most fanatical and loyal collection of supporters in the country.

To follow the Reds in the 1950s was galling in the extreme. For a start, it meant being ridiculed by Evertonians - whose own team was no more than mediocre, albeit in the First Division - and taken for granted by a board apparently devoid of ambition.

There was a whiff of decay over a stagnant Anfield, which languished scruffily, seemingly as uncared-for as an unfashionable seaside resort in winter, while the training ground at Melwood was also in need of improvement.

Naturally enough, the atmosphere communicated itself to the players, and while most of them attained a certain standard through personal and professional pride, there was no guiding hand to lift them towards realising the massive potential of the great institution they served.

Under Taylor, Liverpool had finished third, fourth and then fourth again in the Second Division and in November 1959, with no sign of improvement evident, the strain of constantly failing to secure promotion to the top flight finally became too much for the manager's health and he resigned.

No disrespect is intended to the gentlemanly Bristolian, but his careworn exit paved the way for the club's regeneration. For in his wake came that footballing messiah, Bill Shankly, who transformed the attitude (immediately) and the fortunes (within two years) of the hitherto somnolent Reds.

Staff and stadium were overhauled in short time, the board was shaken from its paralysing apathy and, most important of all, the fans were accorded the respect they deserved.

As Roger put it: 'Bill Shankly sensed what could be achieved and, as a passionate man himself, he felt keenly the passion and the longing of the fans. He believed the club simply wasn't good enough for the people of Liverpool - and said so. It was obvious that Merseysiders and Bill Shankly were meant for each other.

'The change that came over the place was incredible. Where there had been the 'nice' approach of Phil Taylor, now there was this bristling, rasping fellow like James Cagney, who was setting out to conquer the world. Everything changed. Suddenly everyone seemed to be walking about with a new sense of purpose, and then there were the little things. For example, we no longer had training kit with holes in it. Looking after that kind of detail was typical of Bill Shankly and it bred a caring attitude throughout the club. It was a privilege to be part of what followed.'

For the new manager's part, he had no doubt that the 21-year-old Hunt was worthy of a major role in the brave new world of Liverpool FC.

Opposite: Roger's threadbare sweater as he readies himself for training mirrored Liverpool's rather somnolent attitude towards gaining promotion in the late 1950s. Under Bill Shankly, the tatty training gear disappeared along with every last trace of complacency.

At the time of Bill's arrival, the dynamic youngster had scored eight times in 16 League outings and was prospering in a new partnership with the vastly experienced Dave Hickson, a controversial recent signing from Everton. Though the ageing Hickson would not figure in the club's long-term plans, the manager preserved the pairing for the remainder of the season, which ended with each striker netting 21 League goals, Dave in a mere 27 appearances, Roger in 36.

For the younger man it represented a phenomenal return in his first term, not only in the senior side but also as a professional footballer. There was a personal highlight, too, in the third round of the FA Cup when the Reds squeezed past Leyton Orient 2-1 in a thriller at Anfield.

It was Roger's first game in the oldest and most glamorous competition of them all, and he began in sensational style with a goal in the first minute. However, Liverpool were in distinctly sluggish mode and the Londoners claimed a richly deserved equaliser, only for the lad from Glazebury to pop up with a last-minute winner.

This time the headlines proclaimed 'Hunt - The Toast Of Merseyside' and 'What A Start, What A Finish', the sort of approbation calculated to turn many a rookie's head. Not Roger's, though. He remained down-to-earth about the whole episode - a quality that would become typical of the Reds during the great years that lay ahead - and merely set about preparing for the next match.

Promotion would have made it a perfect start for all concerned, but with Shanks gradually easing a whole posse of unwanted players out through the Anfield door while simultaneously addressing the tricky task of replacing them, another third-place finish was deemed acceptable.

Not surprisingly, expectations were sky-high for season 1960/61 and, perhaps understandably during a period of such radical transition, they were not quite met. Liverpool finished third yet again, a hefty six points adrift of promoted Sheffield United, and Shankly was privately devastated.

He had believed Liverpool's wilderness years were at an end but had perhaps under-estimated how hard he would have to strive to make his directors share his vision. For the moment, at least, parsimony still prevailed in the boardroom.

The late, great Bill Shankly, 'founding father' of the modern Liverpool FC and a man whose memory Roger holds in undying affection and respect.

It had proved a frustrating campaign for Roger Hunt, too. He had scored 19 goals in 36 League and Cup outings - by no means a niggardly strike-rate - but had been troubled by a persistent ankle injury which reduced his effectiveness.

However, his overall game was developing apace, thanks in no small measure to the close attention of Shanks and his two lieutenants, Bob Paisley and Reuben Bennett. Roger thrived on the extra ball-work which had been introduced to the training schedule, while his stamina improved significantly.

Also, his aerial work was increasingly productive, which would prove crucial when he became the team's chief spearhead - despite continuing to wear the number-eight shirt - following the departure of Hickson in the spring.

Billy Liddell, too, left at the end of 1960/61, closing a symbolic door on Anfield's recent past. Happily the future, for Roger and the Reds, was laden with promise.

GOAL GLUT

It had been a long time coming, but when it finally arrived in 1961/62 Liverpool's promotion to the First Division was achieved with a rare flourish. Shankly's Reds topped the table by eight points, lifting the title with five matches to spare, and the fast-maturing Roger Hunt contributed a little matter of 41 goals in 41 League appearances.

In retrospect, it all seems so inevitable. A sequence of Division Two finishes which read third, third, fourth, fourth, third and third was surely going to culminate in glory sooner or later.

But somehow, at least to the supporters at the time, it wasn't quite like that. Certainly until Shanks arrived, there was always the niggling doubt that, despite all the potential, the impetus might slip away. After all, what was to prevent other emerging teams from developing more rapidly and condemning the Anfield men to another generation in the doldrums?

Of course, it is doubtful, practically inconceivable, that the possibility of ultimate failure ever crossed the Shankly mind. In 1960/61 he had continued to hone his combination - introducing workaholic wing-half Gordon Milne from Preston North End, recognising the true worth of hitherto overlooked full-back Gerry Byrne, calling to the colours a locally-born teenage winger name of Ian Callaghan and presiding sagely over the continued progress of Roger Hunt.

But it was in the spring and summer of '61, as frustrated fans mulled over yet another failure to join the elite, that Shanks made his most crucial excursions to date into the transfer market.

The purchases of the combative, multi-talented centre-forward Ian St John from Motherwell and Ron Yeats, a veritable man-mountain of a stopper from Dundee United,

Roger celebrates news of his first England call-up by opening the scoring against Rotherham United at Anfield in March 1962. It was his 37th League strike of the campaign, beating the club record for one season set up by Gordon Hodgson in 1935/36.

Roger Hunt and Ian Callaghan, Liverpool team-mates during the 1960s and friends ever since. Roger remembers giving Cally his first pass - and Cally recalls that it was a bad one!

proved the turning point, from both political and playing viewpoints.

Firstly, by arguing his case relentlessly and successfully in the boardroom for the cash to buy them (some £67,500 in total, a fortune at the time), the manager won over certain reluctant directors and established to a wider audience that he and Liverpool really meant business.

Secondly, and of paramount importance to the Kopite legions, the two Scots brought quality and steel to the spine of the side, enabling many of the players around them to blossom fully. One such was Roger Hunt, who revelled in his partnership with the dashing 'Saint', whose penchant for lying deeper than was currently fashionable for a number-nine created acres of forward space for the hard-running Englishman to exploit.

Roger looks back with undisguised relish to a landmark campaign: 'It was a pleasure to play for Liverpool in 1961/62. A goal-scorer can't ask for more than to be part of a good side which believes in going forward and does so at every opportunity. Ian and I gelled straight away. He was a terrific, unselfish player and we seemed to be able to read each other's minds. The fact that he tended to drift back into midfield to pick up the ball early meant I was more an out-and-out striker than a conventional inside-forward, but with two wingers offering super service - Alan A'Court on one side and either Kevin Lewis or Ian Callaghan on the other - that was no hardship.'

The Reds started the season with six straight wins, then drew at Brighton before four more consecutive victories gave them a swingeing, table-topping lead with 21 points from a possible 22. The name of Hunt was dominating the scoresheet with gratifying regularity, with an early hat-trick against Leeds United - the first of five during the campaign - being especially spectacular.

It was a period when everything Roger hit seemed to end up in the net. Long-range thunderbolts were interspersed with routine tap-ins, his head-work proved more prolific than ever, and he was finding time to set up chances for the likes of St John, Jimmy Melia and winger Kevin Lewis.

The plaudits began to rain down, but he remains refreshingly eager to acknowledge that his bounty was merely the end-product of a magnificent team effort, while attributing enormous credit to Shankly.

'He was a great communicator and some of his team talks were fantastic. I remember one when we were about to play his old team, Huddersfield Town - it was hilarious. He went through their team player by player, pulling each individual apart: one was past it, another could never play, another would have been up all night and so on.

'Then he came to Ray Wilson, the England left-back, whom even Bill had to admit was a good footballer but he got round it by saying that Ray was having a bad season. Then he got to Denis Law, whom he glossed over because Denis was always his favourite player. At the end of it all we were left wondering how he could ever have managed such a bad team! Of course, what he was doing really was not pulling them down but building us up. It worked brilliantly and gave us a laugh at the same time.'

Gordon Wallace discovers there is no chance of a peaceful soak with Roger Hunt around. Left to right are Alan A'Court, Jimmy Melia, Roger, Bert Slater, Ian St John, Kevin Lewis, Tommy Leishman and Gordon.

Right: Roger is welcomed to the international scene by Lord Harewood, then a future president of the Football Association, at Wembley in April 1962. The Liverpool sharp-shooter marked his England debut with a goal in the 3-1 victory over Austria. Other players, left to right, are Ron Flowers, John Connelly, Ray Wilson and Jimmy Armfield. On the far left is FA Secretary Sir Stanley Rous.

Below: Roger Hunt of Liverpool and England.

Opposite: Carrying on the good work. Roger hurdles a prone East German defender to score in his second international, in Leipzig in June 1963.

Inevitably as the term progressed, Roger's sharp-shooting attracted the attention of England boss Walter Winterbottom, who was not deterred by the blond marksman's Second Division status. He had never appeared at England schoolboy, youth or under-23 level, so the international stage represented something of a step into the great unknown and Winterbottom eased him in via the Football League, which in those days was virtually the full national side by another name.

It was March 1962 when Roger lined up alongside such household names as Johnny Haynes and Bobby Charlton to face the Scottish League at Villa Park, and while the game ended in a 4-3 defeat, the new boy recorded a personal triumph with two debut goals.

Two weeks later, still only 23 years old, he was rewarded with his first full cap, against Austria at Wembley, and responded in the most appropriate manner, with a goal in a 3-1 victory.

Roger's call-up, which could hardly have been long delayed given his weight of goals in club football, was facilitated by Jimmy Greaves being away on European duty with Tottenham Hotspur.

Thereafter, the names of Greaves and Hunt would be linked frequently in often-stormy debate over the England number-eight shirt, much more of which later. Suffice it to say for the moment that Roger was elated by his elevation to the international ranks, and burning with determination to ensure it was not a one-off occurrence.

Meanwhile, back at Anfield life continued to be unremittingly sweet. The Second Division championship was secured in early April, leaving the final five matches to be played in an atmosphere of carnival, with the fans being treated to a grandstand finish in the last home game against Charlton Athletic.

With only a minute left, the visitors were a goal to the good and it seemed that Anfield would ring down the curtain on an unfitting and untypical note of anti-climax. Enter Roger Hunt with an opportunistic equaliser, followed by Alan A'Court with an improbable last-gasp winner. The Kop's cup of joy overflowed and the seal was set on Shankly's first major managerial achievement; the Reds' last-match reverse at Swansea didn't seem to matter.

In the final reckoning, Roger's 41 Second Division goals made him the League's top scorer and eclipsed the previous Reds record for one season, that of 37 set by Gordon Hodgson in 1935/36. It was a figure no Anfield man would approach over the next quarter of a century; indeed, with modern defenders being fitter and better drilled than their old-time counterparts, it seems unlikely that the mark will ever be passed.

Those seeking to remove some of the gloss from the glory of both Hunt and Liverpool pointed out that it was not gained at the top level. Certain critics even suggested that there had been 'nothing to beat' in the Second Division, but their ungraciousness was exceeded only by their fundamental lack of accuracy.

The opposition included Sunderland, then knocking on the promotion door with a persistence which echoed the Reds' own during previous years, who boasted a rampant Brian Clough as marksman-in-chief; then there was a Stanley Matthews-inspired Stoke City, about to embark on a stirring revival; a Leyton Orient combination which was much underrated and thoroughly merited their runners-up spot, and redoubtable clubs such as Newcastle United and Preston North End, who were not yet debilitated by the recent removal of the maximum wage.

Clearly, then, it was no hollow victory and the men who restored the Merseysiders to the top echelon of English football deserved every morsel of credit which came their way.

The medal-winners were goalkeepers Bert Slater and Jim Furnell (who arrived from Burnley for the last two months of the campaign), full-backs Gerry Byrne, Dick White and Ronnie Moran, half-backs Gordon Milne, skipper Ron Yeats and Tommy Leishman, and forwards Kevin Lewis, Ian Callaghan, Roger Hunt, Ian St John, Jimmy Melia and Alan A'Court.

Now all Roger needed to cap a storybook campaign was selection for England's World Cup party, which was headed for the finals in Chile that summer. Despite his own inexperience and the pressing claims of such worthy rivals such as Ray Crawford of Ipswich Town, Burnley's Ray Pointer and the aforementioned Clough, the call duly came and he jetted off to South America with high hopes.

As it turned out, his sojourn in the sun was to be almost wholly inactive. With strikers such as Greaves, Gerry Hitchens of Inter Milan and Middlesbrough's Alan Peacock ahead of him in the pecking order, he didn't get a look-in, being passed over for all of his country's four games.

The party's base camp was in Coya, a picturesque village high in the mountains from which idyllic setting they would travel down twisted roads bounded by heart-stoppingly precipitous drops to Rancagua for the preliminary group matches, then to Vina del Mar for the quarter-final.

'Although it was like a paid holiday in some ways, with plenty of golf in delightful surroundings and with locals and tourists making us extremely welcome, it was utterly frustrating for me and the other lads who didn't get a game, excellent players such as John Connelly

The genial Walter Winterbottom (left) welcomes Stan Anderson and Roger to the England camp before their international debuts against Austria.

(Burnley), George Eastham (Arsenal), Don Howe and Bobby Robson (WBA), Alan Hodgkinson Sheffield United, Peter Swan (Sheffield Wednesday) and my old chum Stan Anderson (Sunderland).

'The unaccustomed backdrop and the tiny crowds for the group matches, which were played out in an unreal, almost silent atmosphere, made it all seem far removed from the football I knew. There was hardly any local interest and it wasn't until we reached the last eight, in which England lost to Brazil in Vina del Mar, that we felt like we were part of the World Cup. Even then the attendance was only just over 17,000.'

Nevertheless, it was all valuable experience for a young man whose soccer horizons to date had been somewhat limited. It was particularly fascinating for Roger to compare the vastly contrasting managerial styles of his own club boss, the abrasively enthusiastic Shankly, with the more measured approach of the donnish Winterbottom.

He says: 'It wasn't that Walter didn't have passion for the game; he did, though he didn't wear it on his sleeve like Shanks. He thought deeply about football, was extremely knowledgeable and had lots of coaching ideas.

'Walter was an extremely likeable fellow who perhaps didn't instil the same degree of squad discipline as, say, Alf Ramsey did later. Somehow he came across more like an old-fashioned amateur, though that may not be fair on him because he did have the respect of his players and was undoubtedly an able manager.'

Such observations apart, Roger had learned plenty, too, from seeing some of the world's most distinguished players in action, but after being away for a month, he was not sorry to return to Culcheth. His quiet home-town offered ideal surroundings in which to prepare for the imminent challenge of the First Division which lay just a few weeks ahead.

1961-62 - Season of bounty

How Roger Hunt scored 41 goals in 41 League games as Liverpool lifted the Second Division title

Aug 19	Bristol Rovers (a)	won 2-0	(Lewis, Hills og)
Aug 23	Sunderland (h)	won 3-0	(Hunt 2, Lewis)
Aug 26	Leeds United (h)	won 5-0	(Hunt 3, Lewis pen, Melia)
Aug 30	Sunderland (a)	won 4-1	(Hunt 2, St John 2)
Sep 2	Norwich City (a)	won 2-1	(Hunt 2)
Sep 9	Scunthorpe United (h)	won 2-1	(Hemstead og, A'Court)
Sep 16	Brighton (a)	drew 0-0	
Sep 20	Newcastle United (a)	won 2-1	(Milne, Heslop og)
Sep 23	Bury (h)	won 5-0	(Melia 2, St John, Hunt, Lewis)
Sep 30	Charlton Athletic (a)	won 4-0	(Hunt 2, Lewis, St John)
Oct 4	Newcastle United (h)	won 2-0	(Lewis, Hunt)
Oct 7	Middlesbrough (a)	lost 0-2	
Oct 14	Walsall (h)	won 6-1	(Lewis, Melia, Hunt 3, St John)
Oct 21	Derby County (a)	lost 0-2	
Oct 28	Leyton Orient (h)	drew 3-3	(Hunt 2, Leishman)
Nov 4	Preston North End (a)	won 3-1	(Milne, Callaghan, St John)
Nov 11	* Luton Town (h	drew 1-1	(Lewis)
Nov 18	Huddersfield Town (a	won 2-1	(Melia, Hunt)
Nov 25	Swansea Town (h)	won 5-0	(Melia 2, Hunt 3)
Dec 2	Southampton (a)	lost 0-2	
Dec 9	Plymouth Argyle (h)	won 2-1	(A'Court, St John)
Dec 16	Bristol Rovers (h)	won 2-0	(St John, Hunt)
Dec 23	Leeds United (a)	lost 0-1	
Dec 26	Rotherham United (a)	lost 0-1	
Jan 13	Norwich City (h)	won 5-4	(Melia 2, Hunt 2, Scott og)
Jan 20	Scunthorpe United (a)	drew 1-1	(St John)
Feb 3	Brighton (h)	won 3-1	(Byrne, Hunt, St John)
Feb 10	Bury (a)	won 3-0	(Hunt 3)
Feb 24	Middlesbrough (h)	won 5-1	(St John 2, Hunt 3)
Mar 3	Walsall (a)	drew 1-1	(A'Court)
Mar 10	Derby County (h)	won 4-1	(Hunt 2, A'Court, Melia)
Mar 17	Leyton Orient (a)	drew 2-2	(A'Court 2)
Mar 24	Preston North End (h)	won 4-1	(Melia, St John, Hunt 2)
Mar 28	Rotherham United (h)	won 4-1	(Hunt, St John 3)
Mar 31	Luton Town (a)	lost 0-1	
Apr 7	Middlesbrough (h)	drew 1-1	(Hunt)
Apr 21	Southampton (h)	won 2-0	(Lewis 2)
Apr 23	Stoke City (h)	won 2-1	(Moran pen, Melia)
Apr 24	Stoke City (a)	drew 0-0	
Apr 28	Plymouth Argyle (a)	won 3-2	(A'Court, St John, Hunt)
Apr 30	Charlton Athletic (h)	won 2-1	(Hunt, A'Court)
May 4	Swansea Town (a)	lost 2-4	(St John, Hunt)
	* Hunt absent injured		

FA CUP

Jan 6	Chelsea (h)	won 4-3	(St John 2, Hunt, A'Court)
Jan 27	Oldham Athletic (a)	won 2-1	(St John 2)
Feb 17	Preston North End (h)	drew 0-0	
Feb 20	Preston North End (a)	drew 0-0	
Feb 26	Preston North End (n)	lost 0-1	

TESTING THE WATER

Now for the big challenge. Would the pundits who reckoned the Reds would flounder in the top grade be vindicated? Or would Hunt, St John, Yeats and company ram the doubters' words back down their throats?

Early indications were worrying, to say the least, as Liverpool kicked off with three successive League defeats and won only four of their first 16 games. Fans who had waited for more than half a decade to reach the First Division were shuddering at the possibility of an early return to the wilderness, their turbulent state of mind not helped by the spectacle of the 'old enemy' across Stanley Park striding out confidently in what was to prove a successful quest for the Championship.

Roger reflects philosophically that, despite Bill Shankly's often outrageous self-confidence, the players might have been slightly overawed by the step-up in stature.

'We all knew it was going to be more difficult and I knew there was no way I was going to score another 41 goals. That just wasn't realistic. But even though we struggled, Shanks never despaired, at least not in front of the players. He told us we were playing well and that the results would come - and eventually they did.'

A moment to savour for Roger (number eight) as he evades the desperate challenges of Everton goalkeeper Gordon West and centre-half Brian Labone to equalise for Liverpool in the final minute of the Merseyside derby at Goodison Park in September 1962. Everton had the last laugh that season, though; they won the League championship.

One occasion that did lift the early-season anxiety was at Goodison Park in late September. With Everton having been relegated in 1951, then passing newly demoted Liverpool on the way back up in 1954, there had been no Merseyside derby with League points at stake for 11 years. Now the two great rivals were poised to resume what remains surely the most passionate conflict in the English game.

Come the great day, with no fewer than 73,000 fans squeezed inside a pulsating Goodison, all the momentum was with the Blues, who were currently contesting the League leadership with Wolverhampton Wanderers. Sure enough, they went ahead through a controversial (what else?) penalty by Roy Vernon, only for Lewis to equalise for the Reds before the interval.

When Everton reclaimed the lead - through former Red Johnny Morrissey, of all people - their supremacy seemed assured, especially when the clock inched round to 4.40 with no further score. But then, to the ecstatic acclaim of the Anfield contingent, Roger Hunt took it upon himself to rewrite the script.

The plucky A'Court, who had set up the first goal, released one last, desperate cross; the diminutive Lewis outmanoeuvred lanky Brian Labone to nod the ball on and Roger dispatched it gleefully into the Toffeemen's net. In terms of League position that melodramatic late strike secured a much-needed point, but in terms of sheer morale and kudos its value was incalculable, and it is embedded forever in the Hunt memory as one of his most joyful footballing experiences.

'The Merseyside derby means so much to so many people. If we had lost then our supporters would have had to wait six months for a chance of revenge, so to score such an important late goal was an indescribable feeling for me.'

Yet despite that euphoric episode, Liverpool's dismal autumn form showed signs of stretching into the winter and there were wild calls for radical restructuring of the team. But the manager kept faith with most of his promotion line-up, making only two significant alterations, replacing goalkeeper Jim Furnell (who had injured a hand) with Tommy Lawrence and dropping left-half Tommy Leishman in favour of his fellow Scot, Willie Stevenson. The former

Above: Back in the big time in 1962/63, Liverpool made a sluggish start but results picked up with the introduction of reliable goalkeeper Tommy Lawrence and cultured wing-half Willie Stevenson. Left to right, back row: Bob Paisley (trainer), Ronnie Moran, Gordon Milne, Tommy Lawrence, Ron Yeats, Gerry Byrne, Willie Stevenson. Front row: Ian Callaghan, Roger Hunt, Ian St John, Jimmy Melia, Kevin Lewis.

Right: The football season and just about everything else was severely disrupted by The Big Freeze of 1963, but training never stopped. Enjoying themselves in the snow at Melwood are, left to right, 'jockeys' Ian St John, Jimmy Melia and Ian Callaghan aboard Kevin Lewis, Roger Hunt and Alan A'Court.

switch increased solidity at the back, the latter injected more creativity in midfield and, sure enough, there was a dramatic change in the Reds' fortunes.

The turning point came in a 3-3 home thriller with Manchester United, then uncomfortably close to the relegation mire, after which self-belief surged through the Anfielders.

There followed nine consecutive League victories - spread over three months because of The Great Freeze, which brought the game and the whole country to a lengthy standstill - catapulting the club from the lower reaches of the table to the fringe of the title race. Roger contributed 11 goals to this rousing sequence, including a hat-trick against bottom club Leyton Orient, whose troubles in their first season among the elite were not destined to abate.

Roger recalls: 'Once we'd become acclimatised we realised that the First Division was not as formidable as we had thought. Naturally enough, defences were more organised and slicker, and I found myself facing such outstanding individuals as Dave Mackay of Tottenham and Ron Harris of Chelsea, but overall there was no great gulf in ability after all.'

Liverpool's progress was underlined in the spring by holding Champions-elect Everton to a goalless draw, a 5-2 drubbing of Tottenham Hotspur at Anfield on Good Friday, then a 1-0 home victory over Manchester United. But if there was any danger of complacency - pretty unthinkable in any team with which Bill Shankly was involved - it was wiped out comprehensively at White Hart Lane on Easter Monday.

Just three days after Spurs had been humbled, they exacted stunning revenge, tearing the Reds apart to the tune of seven goals to two. That Roger grabbed the Merseysiders' brace was of scant consolation as the Londoners ran amok and a predatory gentleman named Greaves scored four.

'It was an amazing turnaround and there was no logical explanation for it,' muses Roger, seemingly still rather puzzled and even a touch rueful more than 30 years on.'

That result effectively ended Liverpool's lingering title ambitions, but the season remained very much alive for them as they had battled through to the semi-final of the FA Cup.

In later decades, when Wembley became something of a second home to the Reds, their presence at that stage of the competition would have caused no more than routine excitement. But in 1963, unlikely though it may seem to modern fans, Liverpool had never won the FA Cup, so their last-four encounter with Leicester at Hillsborough was billed as one of the most crucial in the club's recent history.

Thus, much was expected of Shankly's men against a team to whom they had already lost twice in the League that term, and in all fairness, the Reds didn't play badly. Though jolted by conceding a first-half goal they proceeded to dominate the game, but were frustrated by a typically dour, though supremely effective performance by the Filberts' rearguard.

Gordon Banks, recently called up for his first appearance between England's posts, was at his most inspired - ironic in view of his less-than-perfect showing against Manchester United in the final - and Liverpool were beaten.

Roger still regards that as the most crushing disappointment of his career, being inflicted as it was by opponents whose rather negative style he disliked, but by season's end both he and his club could look back on an admirable term of consolidation.

He had scored 24 League goals, plus two in the Cup, to underline his credentials as one of the country's top strikers and Liverpool had finished eighth in the table while reaching the FA Cup semi-final.

In addition, though there were no further international opportunities during the domestic season, Roger was summoned by the new England boss, Alf Ramsey, to join a European tour during the summer of 1963. Again he found himself in the shadow of a bang-in-form Jimmy Greaves, but won his second cap when a bout of tonsilitis forced the Spurs man to withdraw from the match with East Germany in Leipzig.

Once more, the whole-hearted Lancastrian made the most of his opening by equalising with a ferocious 20-yard power-drive, then going on to make a competent all-round contribution to his country's ultimate 2-1 victory.

Thus for both Roger Hunt and Liverpool, the springboards to loftier heights were firmly in place. Take-off would not be long delayed.

Right: Ready for the off. Roger and Ian St John ensure they are properly shod for the start of another new season.

Opposite: Roger Hunt never boasted the magical skills of a George Best or a Peter Thompson, but he was no slouch, either!

CARNIVAL TIME

The Anfield faithful could hardly believe their eyes. After a buoyant return to the top flight which had left them fizzing with excitement over prospects for 1963/64, the Reds kicked off the new campaign with three consecutive home defeats.

The fans were dismayed and the players were puzzled, but Bill Shankly professed himself not worried in the slightest. Supported by the evidence of seven points out of eight garnered away from Anfield, he asserted to all and sundry that Liverpool were playing well, that they had been horribly unlucky against Nottingham Forest, Blackpool and West Ham United and that results would turn.

Indeed, after the third setback he announced to his directors, with typically ironic bravado: 'I assure you, gentlemen, that before the end of the season we WILL win a home game!'

As Roger Hunt observes, Shanks could afford to quip about the situation because he knew he was right: 'After getting promotion in 1961/62, then doing well in both League and Cup in the following season, we were confident that we were good enough to win something this time around. Our rotten start didn't dent that confidence because, quite simply, it was genuine.'

Wolves discovered just how genuine when - complete with star centre-forward Ray Crawford, making his first appearance since his much-trumpeted transfer from Ipswich Town - they arrived at Anfield with something of a swagger. They departed in rather more subdued mood after being trounced 6-0 by the rampant Reds, with Roger striking twice to maintain a run of prolific personal form.

Though the next game brought another reverse, at the hands of Sheffield United at Bramall Lane, there followed nine victories from ten matches and a challenge for the title began to seem conceivable. The side, bolstered by the £40,000 arrival of the hugely gifted winger Peter Thompson from Preston North End during the summer, was functioning with

Family scenes from the sixties.
Right: Roger passes on a few tricks
of the trade to his son, David, who
keeps his eyes firmly on the ball in
the best Hunt tradition. Below:
David and his little sister, Julie,
watch the birdie.

smooth efficiency, though some injury-induced tinkering around mid-term produced even more impressive results.

Jimmy Melia was sidelined by an ankle injury and there was no obvious replacement for the skilful midfield general. Accordingly, Shanks came up with a shrewd reshuffle, withdrawing the creative Ian St John into an even deeper role than usual and pitching Alf Arrowsmith, a raw, engagingly enthusiastic young charger, into the front line alongside Roger.

So effective did the new combination prove, with Arrowsmith scoring heavily, that the unfortunate Melia, still only 25 despite being a first-team regular since the mid-1950s, found himself out in the cold. Before long, seeing little future for himself with his home-town club, the popular, prematurely balding Scouser left to join Wolves.

The Reds continued to pile up the points but, as Roger recalls, it was Easter before the players' thoughts turned towards a possible title challenge: 'Until then we'd spent most of our time in fifth or sixth position and were regarded as rank outsiders, but a six-point Easter against stiff opposition changed all that.'

On Good Friday, a memorable Hunt hat-trick secured a crucial 3-1 victory over Championship hopefuls Tottenham at White Hart Lane. Twenty four hours later Leicester City, who had become Liverpool's bogey team in recent seasons, were put to the sword at Filbert

Above: Friends and rivals. Roger menaces the West Ham goal but is foiled by Martin Peters, alongside whom he was destined to scale the giddiest of heights for England. In close attendance is their international skipper, Bobby Moore, while the anxious Hammers custodian is Jim Standen.

Overleaf: Sir Roger in full cry. Tottenham full-back Ron Henry is left trailing as the Liverpool marksman cracks the ball past goalkeeper John Hollowbread. Hunt's Good Friday hat-trick at White Hart Lane was the start of a happy Easter which saw the Reds close in on the Championship.

Street, then Spurs crashed 3-1 at Anfield on Easter Monday.

Suddenly the Reds were favourites and their next match was against Manchester United, the only club with a realistic chance of overhauling them. By now Matt Busby had almost finished rebuilding his team in the wake of the Munich air disaster; Bobby Charlton and Denis Law were in or approaching their prime, George Best was emerging from the wings and the Red Devils were almost ready to reach out for another League title. But, as they discovered in front of more than 52,000 fans at a seething Anfield, almost is not quite.

United were put firmly in their place by one of their own, the Mancunian Arrowsmith scoring twice in a 3-0 win that left Liverpool on the brink of lifting the domestic game's premier prize only two years after rising from the Second Division.

Roger, however, was in a state of rare anxiety. An ankle injury ruled him out of the following game, in which Burnley were swept aside at Turf Moor, and with only two points needed for the Championship he feared he might miss out on the biggest celebration of his career to date.

'Our next game was against Arsenal at Anfield, and Bill Shankly didn't seem to mind whether I played or not. Gordon Wallace, of whom he thought so highly that he had likened

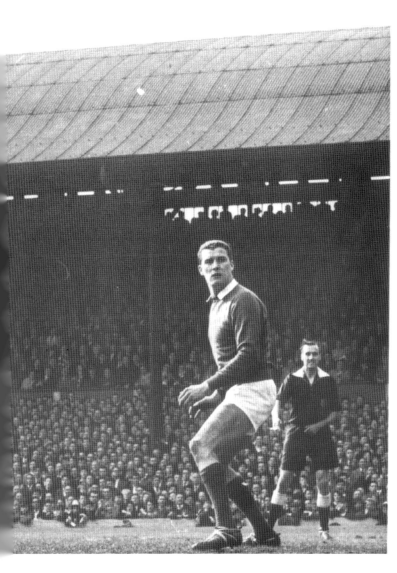

him to a young Tom Finney, had done well as my replacement against Burnley and was all ready to continue.

'I shall never forget the morning of that match. I was still feeling twinges from my sore ankle but I couldn't bear the thought of missing out at the death so I declared fit and was in. It was a beautiful, sunny, spring day, the sort when it feels good just to be alive, and as the ground filled up the crowd were in high spirits.'

Truly it was an occasion to savour and the match turned out to be something of a carnival, complete with procession! St John eased any vestige of nerves with an early goal, Tommy Lawrence rattled the Gunners' comeback hopes by saving a George Eastham penalty, then Arrowsmith joined the party with a goal just before the interval.

The second half was a Liverpool beanfeast, with Thompson scoring twice and Roger once to make it 5-0 after an hour, leaving the Reds to coast joyously towards the final whistle and that coveted trophy. Ian Callaghan was left as the only home forward not to find the net after former team-mate Jim Furnell saved his spot-kick, but that was an insignificant detail to an Anfield awash with euphoria.

The Kopites had been starved of success for so long and now they were gorging them-

selves on glory. As well as jubilation, there was an outpouring of relief that the Reds had raised themselves triumphantly from the gloomy pit of mediocrity that had gripped them in the pre-Shankly era, a similar tidal wave of emotion to the one that engulfed Old Trafford when United clinched the League Championship after a 26-year wait in 1993.

Roger reminisces: 'It was one of the most fantastic days of my life. The happiness on people's faces had to be seen to be believed. It was all part of a fantastic period in the city of Liverpool, what with the Beatles emerging at the same time. Whichever way you looked there was something happening.

'We had won the League and we had won it well, playing attractive attacking football and using our two wingers to full advantage. I can't believe there has been a better club pairing than Ian and Peter anywhere. Some of our critics, especially those down south, said we were too much like a machine, that our game was predictable and boring, but the players paid no attention to that - they knew it wasn't true.'

This evidence of mental fortitude was allied to immense physical strength and resilience. Roger continues: 'Bill Shankly used to say we were the fittest side in the League and he was probably right. We scored a lot of goals very late in games because we could keep going when others were flagging. Even if they had as much skill as us, they didn't have the strength left to make it count.

'Our training was creative and nearly all of it was done with the ball. There was lots of close-quarters, short-passing stuff, two-a-side in a small boarded box. The beauty of it was that it continually threw up match-type situations where you'd receive the ball in a confined space, then have to move or pass immediately - that's what the Liverpool style of football was all about. You'd be on your knees at the end of every session, but it was invaluable.'

Roger found Shankly's way contrasted vividly with the methods employed during the reign of Phil Taylor: 'Before Shanks arrived we did not see too much of the ball in training. The idea was that it made you more hungry for it on match day. That's not to single out Phil Taylor for criticism, it's just the way it was at most clubs in those days.

'But Shanks preached that you used the ball to make your living, so you must be as familiar with it as possible. He would tell us time and again that it was the most important tool of our trade.'

Roger had scored 31 of the Reds' 92 League goals in 1963/64 and had reason for immense personal satisfaction, but there was never any chance of his getting carried away with his own importance. Apart from his own natural modesty, he was also subject to the same feet-on-the-ground regime that governed everyone at the club.

He explains: 'No one got big-headed at Liverpool. That sort of behaviour would have been stamped out before it could take hold. Shanks, Bob Paisley, Reuben Bennett and Joe Fagan were all of a mind on that. Liverpool was a no-frills club and if you reached the top you were expected to work to stay there, not waste time crowing about it.'

With that thrashing of Arsenal, the Reds HAD reached the top, yet there was still an element of disappointment at the end of a remarkable season. After losing in the last four of the FA Cup the previous year, then seeing off Arsenal to reach the quarter-final in 1964, the Merseysiders had a gut feeling that they were Wembley-bound at last.

That impression was not lessened when they were paired with Swansea Town, then struggling near the foot of the Second Division, especially with the tie being at Anfield. But come the day they ran into a goalkeeper playing the game of his life and lost 2-1 in one of the great Cup upsets of the decade.

Roger still winces as he recalls the performance of Republic of Ireland international Noel Dwyer: 'I had never seen anything like it. He made a whole series of phenomenal saves, catching shots that he had no right even to get near. Luck went his way, too - there were several occasions when he dived one way and the ball went the other, only to hit his legs and rebound to safety - but, in all fairness, he deserved his rub of the green. To make matters worse, Ronnie Moran missed a penalty for us, but nobody blamed him. We all felt sorry for him.

'After that defeat we thought we'd probably NEVER win the Cup.'

Little did they know how wrong they were, or how short their wait would be!

Opposite above: In those lovely, far-off days when most pitch invasions were no more than spontaneous expressions of joy, a Liverpool fan tells Roger Hunt what a jolly fine fellow he is. And why not? The Reds have just clinched the League title with a glorious annihilation of Arsenal. Ian Callaghan and Tommy Lawrence (far right) lead the triumphant procession around a delirious Anfield.

Opposite below: Bubbly time back in the dressing room. Celebrating in style are (stood on a bench at the back, left to right) Ronnie Moran, Gerry Byrne and Ian Callaghan. With their feet more or less on the ground are, from the left, Alf Arrowsmith, Roger Hunt, Gordon Milne, Ian St John, Tommy Lawrence, Peter Thompson, Willie Stevenson, Bill Shankly, trainer Reuben Bennett and a besuited Chris Lawler.

THE BEST YET

Liverpool began season 1964/65 as Champions, but uneasy was the head that wore the crown, despite a first-day fillip in a pulsating contest chosen by the BBC as their inaugural *Match Of The Day*. On August 22, the television cameras were at Anfield for the visit of Billy Wright's Arsenal and just 11 minutes into the life of what would become a national institution, Roger Hunt made his mark.

Peter Thompson bemused former England full-back and future Highbury boss Don Howe on the left and dispatched a deep cross which reached Ian Callaghan on the opposite flank. Little Cally, an ever-growing force destined to be one of the Reds' greatest players, controlled the ball cleverly on his chest before dinking it towards but slightly behind Roger, lurking unmarked near the penalty spot.

There seemed little immediate danger as the ball was arriving at an awkward height and angle, but the England marksman displayed his burgeoning class. Swivelling adroitly, he sent a gentle but exquisitely placed volley looping beyond Jim Furnell into the far corner of the net. Kenneth Wolstenholme purred, the Kop went wild and Saturday nights would never be the same again.

It was an auspicious beginning, both for *MoD* and Liverpool's new campaign, but although the home team claimed victory on that warm summer day, winning 3-2 thanks to a brace of goals from Gordon Wallace, an autumn of unexpected travail was in prospect.

Shankly's side won only three of their next 15 League matches, allowing the title to slide beyond their realistic reach at a sickenly early stage of its defence. Indeed, they were to finish in a deflating seventh position, 17 points behind champions Manchester United, though there were extenuating circumstances.

One small step for Liverpool, one gigantic leap for football coverage on TV. Roger Hunt takes centre stage in an exciting moment from the Reds' First Division encounter with Arsenal at Anfield on Saturday, August 22, 1964. For Bill Shankly's team it represented a victorious start to the season; for the football-loving world at large it went down in history as the BBC's first Match Of The Day. For the record, Liverpool won 3-2 with Roger grabbing the first goal.

Above: Ron Yeats tickles the ivories as the Reds sing along with Shirley Bassey, one of the many celebrities they met as they became ever more famous themselves. Behind Big Ron, left to right, are Tommy Lawrence, Gerry Byrne, Ronnie Moran, Tommy Smith, Alf Arrowsmith, Geoff Strong and Roger Hunt. Ian St John and Gordon Milne (far right) are hogging the limelight at the front.

Left: Roger is on the end of some good-natured banter after receiving a newspaper award. His team-mates are, left to right, Willie Stevenson, Peter Thompson, Gerry Byrne, Ian St John, Tommy Smith, Ian Callaghan and Ron Yeats.

As the shadows lengthen on an autumn afternoon at Anfield in 1964, Roger Hunt shoots for goal against West Ham. Somehow, it's a picture that sums up the appeal of football in general, and Liverpool in particular, during that narvellous, vibrantly exciting era. Oblivious to their participation in a slice of nostalgia are the Reds' Bobby Graham (left) and Hammers' defenders John Bond (centre) and Eddie Bovington.

Ian St John, a crucially constructive (and competitive) component of the team, spent the first three weeks of the season recovering from appendicitis, while Alf Arrowsmith, so prolific the previous term, had succumbed to a serious injury and would never be the same again. Also there was the little matter of the club's first European campaign, which had started well but inevitably proved something of a distraction.

Meanwhile Roger was maintaining his personal form splendidly, his 15 League goals before Christmas representing a more-than-reasonable return for a striker in an off-the-boil side.

Of course, such is the beauty of English club football that, come the new year, League disappointments can be pushed momentarily to one side while compensation is sought in the FA Cup. So it was at Anfield, where the pursuit of that particular trophy had become something of an obsession.

As mentioned earlier, Liverpool had never won the Cup. In fact, they had been to only two finals, losing to Burnley in 1914 and Arsenal in 1950, and the supporters now talked openly of some mischievous jinx barring their path to what remained to many the most prestigious club prize.

If they believed that, there was evidence in the third-round victory at West Bromwich Albion to suggest that the bogey was about to be laid. Goals from Roger and the 'Saint' secured a 2-1 triumph, but only after an almost surreal incident when Liverpool captain Ron Yeats, believing he had heard the referee's whistle, picked up the ball with his hands in mid penalty area. To Ron's horror, the blast had come from a mischievous fan and a spot-kick was awarded. However, justice was done when Bobby Cram missed from 12 yards.

Stockport County at Anfield in the fourth round presented what seemed like a formality, so much so that Bill Shankly missed the match, flying to Germany to vet the Reds' forthcoming European Cup opponents, FC Cologne. Back at the airport on his return, he asked a customs officer the score and was rendered speechless (well, almost!) on hearing that the humble visitors had held his Reds to 1-1. His first words on being reunited with his players have not been recorded, perhaps fortunately so. But whatever injunctions he issued had the desired effect, Liverpool dominating the replay on a sandy surface reminiscent of Southport beach and going through on the back of two Hunt strikes.

A tight fifth-round contest with Bolton Wanderers at Burnden Park, throughout much of which Yeats limped courageously to contain the fearsome aerial threat of Wyn 'The Leap' Davies, was decided by a late goal from Cally. Roger recalls: 'It was a header and he didn't get many of those. He came in for a tremendous ribbing from the lads, and quite right too!'

Cally's timely decider set up a fascinating quarter-final clash with old adversaries Leicester City at Filbert Street, and Roger admits there were plenty of groans in the Liverpool dressing-room when the tie was announced.

'They had given us so much trouble in the past that they were just about the last opponents we would have chosen. We were pleased to draw 0-0 in an extremely tense game at Leicester, but we knew that didn't guarantee our passage. Back in October they had beaten us with a breakaway goal at Anfield and were clearly extremely dangerous to our Cup prospects.

'To be honest, they could have won the replay. It was very even, with good chances missed at both ends, and I was so relieved to score with only 18 minutes left. I shall remember that goal as long as I live. Chris Lawler hoisted a free-kick into their box, Ron Yeats nodded it down and I hit a left-foot volley from the edge of the area. It kept low, beat Gordon Banks, smacked against the stanchion and bounced back out. It was a fantastic feeling and I can relive the excitement when I think back to it now.

'I thought those last few minutes would never tick away. There had been so many tough meetings with Leicester that a bit of feeling had crept in. They had some very fine, very competitive players - people such as Frank McLintock, Davy Gibson and Mike Stringfellow - and manager Matt Gillies had them organised to perfection. Their method wasn't particularly pretty but there was no one like them for soaking up pressure. That made this win very, very sweet.'

As morale-boosters go, then, Liverpool couldn't have asked for better, but pessimistic

pundits reckoned that their chances against Chelsea in the semi-final took a hefty jolt when, only three days ahead of the Villa Park encounter, the Reds were forced into extra time in a replay against FC Cologne played on a stamina-sapping mudpatch in neutral Rotterdam.

Roger recollects: 'Tommy Docherty, the Chelsea manager, was as pleased as punch. He thought we'd be exhausted and he reckoned his exciting young side were ideal to take advantage.

'But Shanks and Bob Paisley were too wily for him. Normally we tried to beat teams by incessant attacking, but this time they advised us to conserve our energy by letting the ball do the work. We played some lovely football that day, the sort of fluid passing game that the club became famous for later, and it paid off.'

Yet for all their poise and precision, the Reds had to wait until after the hour before man-of-the-match Peter Thompson put them in front with a scintillating goal. A Willie Stevenson penalty near the end confirmed their superiority.

The stage was now set for the Wembley final against Leeds United, a contest which assumed mammoth proportions on Merseyside as the great day neared. Roger had never known the public's expectations so high and it was a tribute to Shankly that he used that

Beer in the bath for Liverpool's players at Villa Park in the spring of 1965. They had earned it by beating Chelsea in an FA Cup semi-final, to set up a Wembley meeting with Leeds United. Left to right are Ian St John, Willie Stevenson, Chris Lawler, Ron Yeats, Roger Hunt, Gordon Milne and Tommy Lawrence.

avalanche of avid anticipation to motivate his men and bolster their self-belief when it could easily have placed them under intolerable pressure.

'Shanks was unbelievable. He seemed to tune in to the total confidence of the fans and it rubbed off on us,' says Roger. 'He was even the subject of *Desert Island Discs* during the week of the match. Of course, he chose all the Kop's favourite songs and everyone loved it.

'To me at the time, getting to Wembley seemed like the absolute peak of my playing life. After all, it's every footballer's ambition. I'd already experienced winning the League and I looked at European competition as a bonus; now an FA Cup winner's medal was what I wanted most of all.'

Yet despite all the euphoria, it was clear that Leeds would not offer themselves up as sacrificial lambs at Wembley. In their first season after promotion to the top flight Don Revie's men had missed the League title only on goal average and they had gained a reputation as an immensely efficient and physically formidable outfit.

Despite all his larger-than-life kidology in the media, the Liverpool boss was well aware of the genuine menace constituted by the ultra-professional Yorkshiremen. Accordingly, he contributed one of his most inspired pre-match talks, rasping with a fervour that did not brook uncertainty: 'You're going to win because you're the best team. Leeds are honoured to be on the same field as you. AND you're not going to disappoint the greatest supporters in the world. If necessary - and it won't be - you should be prepared to die for them.'

The Reds who strode out to battle on a dank, miserable Wembley afternoon, those stirring words still ringing in their ears, were Tommy Lawrence, Chris Lawler, Gerry Byrne, Ron Yeats, Tommy Smith (who wore the number 10 on his back but played alongside his captain at the back), Geoff Strong, Willie Stevenson, Ian Callaghan, Roger Hunt, Ian St John and Peter Thompson. Poor Gordon Milne was confined to a watching brief on the bench, having been injured in a League game two weeks earlier, but Strong was a more-than-able midfield deputy.

Facing them, still smarting from their narrow failure to lift the Championship, were goalkeeper Gary Sprake, full-backs Paul Reaney and Willie Bell, half-backs Billy Bremner, Jack Charlton and Norman Hunter and a forward line of Johnny Giles, Jim Storrie, Alan Peacock, skipper and Footballer of the Year Bobby Collins and Albert Johanneson.

Within three minutes of the start, Gerry Byrne could have been excused for wondering whether his manager's 'do-or-die' imprecation was to be taken literally. The wholehearted left-back had broken his collarbone in a collision with the tiny but unrelentingly fierce Collins, and though he was not instantly aware of the extent of his injury, the pain from the two edges of bone grinding together with every movement must have been excruciating. Incredibly, he was to soldier on through a further 117 minutes of action, and whatever else came to pass on Wembley's rain-slicked surface, he was the day's real hero.

In all honesty, as a spectacle for neutral spectators the match was a letdown, being labelled 'Bore of the Roses' by uncharitable headline-writers. Roger admits that for most of its length it produced stultifying stalemate, Liverpool pouring forward but lacking the necessary cutting edge to unsettle a Leeds combination dedicated to stout defence with the occasional counter-attack.

It was three minutes into extra time that the deadlock was shattered, and Roger was the man to do it. Leeds legs were finally tiring as Willie Stevenson, by common consent the most effective man afield, drifted past two weary challenges and released the ball to the iron-willed Byrne, who could still muster the energy to storm down the left flank.

Roger takes up the narrative: 'Gerry reached the byline and got in a low, firm cross, which by-passed Sprake on the near post. Charlton and the winger Giles, whose presence in the goalmouth showed the extent to which Leeds were being pressed back, were close by but I was on my own just a few yards out as the ball reached me at about waist height. At first, I didn't know whether to head it or side-foot it. I went for the header, having to stoop slightly, and I was absolutely overjoyed to watch it go in.'

The scorer, his team-mates, the travelling Kopites and the watching world thought that was that. After Liverpool had probed for so long to break down their stubborn opponents'

The moment Roger Hunt thought he had sealed the first FA Cup triumph in Liverpool's history. As he stoops to nod the ball into Leeds' unguarded net, it appears that Ian Callaghan (left) and Ian St John (right) share his opinion. In fact, Don Revie's men still had a trick up there sleeves, but it all worked out right for the Reds in the end.

Enjoying the game . . . tension on the front bench during the 1965 FA Cup Final as the downpour intensifies. Left to right are the Liverpool contingent of Bob Paisley, Reuben Bennett, the injured Gordon Milne and Bill Shankly; next comes a ball boy, presumably a neutral; and then the Leeds party, comprising Syd Owen, Don Revie (doing a fair impression of a gibbering wreck) and Les Cocker.

distinctly negative tactics, it seemed inconceivable that one breakthrough would not be enough to claim the spoils.

Leeds, however, were made of undeniably stern stuff and eight minutes later they equalised with a brilliantly executed snap-shot from the irrepressible Billy Bremner. Says Roger: 'It was stunning, we just hadn't expected it. Having seemingly won it once, now we had to win it all over again.'

And that's what they did. Shrugging off the shock, the Reds continued to rampage forward and nine minutes from time, Cally slipped the hitherto clamlike attentions of Willie Bell to

break free on the right. His raking cross was met by a thrillingly airborne St John, whose bullet header inscribed Liverpool's name on the FA Cup for the first time.

Roger, by no means an over-emotional individual, was unashamedly moved by the ecstatic reaction of the Scouse hordes at the final whistle. The sound was earth-shaking, even by Kop standards, as the bedraggled, scarlet-shirted victors paraded the trophy around the stadium.

Typically, amidst the bedlam of celebration, Roger spared a thought for fellow England international Gordon Milne. Drenched by the downpour, the sidelined wing-half had swapped

Parading the spoils of a hard-fought victory over Leeds at Wembley in 1965. Revelling in their lap of honour, despite the rain, are (left to right) Ian St John, Ian Callaghan, Chris Lawler, Tommy Smith, Tommy Lawrence, Roger Hunt, the courageous Gerry Byrne and man-of-the-match Willie Stevenson.

his natty lounge suit for a tracksuit at the interval, but retained his soggy suede shoes as he shared in the lap of honour.

'I felt sorry for Gordon. He had been with us all the way, only to miss out when we reached the climax. He put a brave face on it, but he must have been suffering inside.'

If the Wembley jollifications proved uproarious enough, they were nothing to what awaited the team on their return to Liverpool the next day. An estimated quarter of a million people lined the route from Lime Street railway station to the town hall and around 90 of them needed treatment after being caught in the crush.

Even Bill Shankly, not a man to be overawed easily, admitted: 'It was a great welcome, but it really put the wind up me.' As for Roger, he was overwhelmed: 'It was a truly incredible experience. The fantastic enthusiasm of those fans underlined to me that playing a part in bringing the Cup back to Anfield ranked as my greatest achievement at the time. Even in the light of what happened afterwards, I'm not sure that I ever topped it.'

It was a time of unrestrained rejoicing in the Hunt household. Three weeks before the final, Roger had become a father for the second time with the birth of Julie. Not that he had much time to relax with his new daughter and six-year-old son, David. Just three days after Wembley, Liverpool's footballers had a rather important appointment at Anfield - a little matter of entertaining Inter Milan in the semi-final of the European Cup.

CONTINENTAL COMPLIMENT

It was, according to Helenio Herrera, a truly exceptional goal. On further reflection, Inter's inimitable coach, a voluble fanatic whom some saw as an Italian version of Shankly himself, wanted to extend the compliment. It was, he continued, a Continental type of goal and he, of all people, couldn't offer higher praise than that.

The recipient of this extravagant bouquet from a renowned adversary whom Shanks had dubbed 'a remarkable little fellow, a cut-throat man who always wants to win', was Roger Hunt. The goal in question was Liverpool's opener after four minutes of what was arguably their finest-ever European performance.

But before describing Roger's coruscating strike in detail, it is appropriate to set the scene. Of course, Anfield had known remarkable nights before, and there have been no shortage of gala occasions since, but it is doubtful whether the famous ground's rafters have been rattled quite so rapturously as on the evening when the European Cup holders came to town.

Consider the circumstances: three days earlier, Liverpool had broken their historical mould of FA Cup failure and were bringing home the trophy to parade before the passionate masses. As a bonus, the Reds were entertaining the Continent's crack side, against whom the more objective of pundits gave them only a limited chance of success. There was, therefore, everything to gain and, with silverware already on the sideboard, no chance of finishing the season empty-handed.

It was a scenario made for the opportunist Shankly - who might have been a professional psychologist had he not been a football manager - and how he capitalised on it!

Having noted the fever pitch of excitement that had built up inside the stadium prior to the start, he ensured that the Italians should take to the pitch first. As they walked out they were greeted by a raw, aggressive cacophony of sound that increased in intensity as they made the mistake of heading for the Kop end.

Belatedly absorbing the message, they turned on their heels and made for the Anfield Road goal, just as Ron Yeats led Liverpool out of the tunnel. That was the signal for the most raucous roar yet. Finally, just as the shell-shocked Milanese must have been longing for kick-off to focus their attention on the job in hand, the manipulator supreme pulled his final and most wily stroke.

Into the arena marched Gordon Milne and Wembley hero Gerry Byrne, brandishing between them the FA Cup, and the noise-level shot off the decibel-meter. The two walking wounded set off on a circuit of the ground which provoked eardrum-shattering delirium in stand and on terrace alike.

A dignified study of Liverpool's first soccer 'knight': Sir Roger at Anfield.

Thus Shanks and the fans had done their part in softening up the visitors; now it was down to the players, and they responded nobly. A mere 240 seconds into the game, the faithful Callaghan supplied an awkwardly bouncing cross which reached Roger some 12 yards out from goal; instinctively, the Liverpool spearhead spun on the spot to crack a pulverising volley into Inter's net, then punched the air in the sheer joy of executing a difficult skill to perfection.

The goal that told the European champions that they were in for a rare old battle: Roger Hunt swivels to hook home a cross from Ian Callaghan against Inter Milan at Anfield.

Roger recalls: 'I've got to admit that was one of my sweetest ever, and it was particularly satisfying as it fitted in so well with the manager's plans. He told us the Italians would come strutting, full of self-belief, and he wanted us to go at them with a wave of early attacks. The crowd was alight and everything fell into place.'

However, barely had the impact of Hunt's 'Continental goal' had time to sink in when the European Champions were level. Their score was brilliant, too, though in a contrasting manner to their hosts'.

'They just played the ball from one end of the pitch to the other without a Liverpool player making contact. It was stunning and showed just what they were capable of. When Mazzola turned the ball into the net the ground, which had been so noisy, was suddenly quiet. It was quite eerie,' remembers the Reds' scorer.

To their huge credit, Liverpool refused to be unsettled by Milan's devastating and rapid riposte, continuing to carry the game to their illustrious visitors and reaping the benefit after 34 minutes. Cally put them back in front following a slick free-kick routine involving Willie Stevenson and Roger: 'Willie took the kick, I touched it on and Cally appeared from nowhere to side-foot it home from a narrow angle. We had practised it a lot and it's always satisfying when something like that works in a match. There's so much that could have gone wrong: Willie's pass might have been inaccurate, I might have miscontrolled it, Ian might not have timed his run properly - but not this time, it was marvellous.'

For the remainder of the contest Liverpool had Inter on the rack, creating numerous chances but making only one of them count, when St John tucked away a Hunt shot that rebounded invitingly. 'We knew we could and should have had more goals, but at 3-1 we felt confident of reaching the final,' remembers Roger. Sadly, it was not to be.

When Liverpool arrived in Italy for the second leg, they discovered that they could not claim any monopoly on rabidly partisan supporters or psychological attrition. Throughout their stay they were abused by Italian fans, who attempted to keep them awake in their hotel by maintaining a continuous all-night din, employing anything from car horns to road drills, and they were vilified and libelled in the press.

That was nothing, though, to the seething cauldron of unbridled bile that was the San Siro stadium as they took to the field. Waves of hysterical hate poured from every tier of the stadium, bonfires were lit on the terraces and, worst of all, potentially lethal rockets were launched horizontally across the pitch. Through amazing good fortune, no one was hurt, but that was all the luck Liverpool were to have that night.

Heartbreakingly after their sterling efforts at Anfield, they found themselves two down inside nine minutes, with both goals the result of horrendous refereeing decisions. First Corso scored with a free-kick the Reds believed to be awarded unjustly and which in any case had been indirect. Then Peiro punted the ball from Tommy Lawrence's grasp as the 'keeper was bouncing it and popped it into the empty net.

Roger shakes his head ruefully at the memory: 'I don't like to make excuses, but on the Continent in those days you couldn't even breathe on the 'keeper without being penalised - and the referee had certainly signalled that free-kick as indirect.

'It ruined our game-plan immediately; we had intended to remove their sting by keeping everything tight early on. Once they were level they had too much nous for us and, to be fair, scored a tremendous winning goal through Facchetti. They had plenty of magnificent players and controlled the match in the end, but the controversial refereeing left a nasty taste.

'We just had to put it down as a bad night. It certainly wasn't enough to sour what had been a wonderful season, though the FA Cup and the European Cup would have made a fantastic double,' he adds wistfully.

During the course of Liverpool's first Continental campaign, Roger had excelled. He had scored three in the opening tie against the charming Icelandic part-timers of Reykjavik, then netted in both meetings with the classy thoroughbreds of Anderlecht. Indeed, particularly in the away leg against the Belgians, he showed intelligent appreciation of the need for a visiting striker to forage alone, as well as the ceaseless, selfless application needed to make a success of the role.

Pints all round when the Reds relax: left to right, Gordon Milne, Geoff Strong and Roger Hunt.

We're all going on a summer holiday . . . taking their ease in Spain are, left to right, Gerry Byrne, Roger Hunt, Joe Fagan (he would never have worn that hat at Melwood), Bob Paisley, club chairman Sid Reakes and Reuben Bennett.

He scored, too, in the quarter-final replay against FC Cologne - which was decided agonisingly, but in the Reds' favour, by the flip of a coloured disc - and was earning a reputation as one of Europe's most formidable front-runners.

Small wonder, then, that stories of various top foreign clubs making Roger a transfer target began to circulate. He says: 'As far as I was concerned it was never anything more than rumours and newspaper talk. Certainly, nothing was ever put to me officially.'

And if it had been? 'I don't think I would have fancied it. I have always liked my home comforts and things were going very well with Liverpool in the mid-1960s, when these whispers got about.'

It was a typically loyal and pragmatic response, exactly what Reds fanatic Stan Green and his Kopite friends would have expected of their mate-next-door hero, but which it would have been wrong to take for granted. Both the club and its fans could consider themselves fortunate.

TOP OF THE CHARTS

Come season 1965/66 and Bill Shankly's first great side were at their height. Employing a mere 14 players, Liverpool won the League Championship, eclipsing nearest challengers Leeds United and Burnley by six points, and reached the final of the European Cup Winners' Cup, losing to Borussia Dortmund only by an astonishing goal in extra time.

The title triumph completed a fabulous treble spread over three successive campaigns - Championship, FA Cup and Championship again - which left Kopites reeling with delight after what had seemed an eternity in the wilderness.

As Roger Hunt puts it, with characteristic lack of embellishment: 'We were a very good side by 1966. We had the benefits of experience, success and togetherness and were getting the rewards.

'Off the pitch we were all very friendly. I was especially close to Cally, Tommy Lawrence, Geoff Strong and Gerry Byrne, while the Scottish lads - Ron Yeats, the 'Saint' and Willie Stevenson - tended to stick together, but there were no real cliques.

'On the pitch, our game was more controlled, there was not so much charging into attack with gay abandon and the defence was much tighter than ever before.'

A very good team indeed: Liverpool in the mid 1960s. Left to right, back row: Gordon Milne, Gerry Byrne, Tommy Lawrence, Willie Stevenson, Chris Lawler. Front row: Ian Callaghan, Roger Hunt, Ron Yeats (skipper), Ian St John, Tommy Smith, Peter Thompson.

The situation is hopeless for prone goalkeeper Tony Waiters as Roger scores against Blackpool at Anfield in February 1966. The strike helped seal a fourth consecutive victory for the Reds, who were on their way to another League title.

For Roger personally, it had been a supremely satisfying campaign, despite niggling ankle injuries at its beginning and end. In 37 League outings he had netted 30 times to top the First Division goal charts and could claim the unusual distinction that his team had won all of the 19 games in which he had scored.

He was, however, beginning to feel some of the strain that life at the summit can bring, especially as the team still didn't contain another specialist striker.

He explains: 'I carried a great personal scoring burden. I loved scoring, and I did score plenty that season, but that responsibility brings its own pressures. If you go four or five games without a goal, then no matter how well you might be playing in general, the press will be talking about what a lean time you're having.'

Roger's first two strikes of 1965/66 had come in a 3-1 victory at Leicester on the opening day - 'a splendid omen,' he smiles - and he had hit the target 19 times by early December. There were scintillating team performances in the 5-1 drubbing of West Ham United at Upton Park and the 5-0 annihilation of Everton in the Anfield derby, but it was not until the turn of the year that the Reds really began to dominate.

Then, after a 1-0 win at Elland Road on December 28 - crucial revenge for a single-goal home defeat by Don Revie's men a day earlier - they shifted up a gear, dropping only one point in their next eight games and being beaten only twice more before season's end.

The FA Cup brought disappointment in the form of an Anfield knockout by Chelsea in the third round, but the Cup Winners' Cup offered stirring compensation. Italian giants Juventus, the combative Standard Liege of Belgium and the famous Hungarian side, Honved, were all seen off on the way to a mouth-watering semi-final confrontation with Glasgow Celtic.

Unfortunately, Roger was struggling with his ankle problem at the time, missing four League games as well as being forced out of both clashes with Jock Stein's 'Bhoys'. He had been stretching to reach a pass during the home encounter with Sheffield Wednesday when he had been clipped accidentally by Gerry Young, a popular fellow who was to endure a particularly traumatic climax to his own season. Gerry it was who dropped the Wembley clanger, screened over and over again on television, which enabled Derek Temple to win the FA Cup for Everton.

Back with the so-called 'Championship of Britain', Liverpool overcame the Celts 2-1 on aggregate to earn a place in the final against the powerful and efficient Borussia Dortmund.

Now Roger faced a race to be fit and when he returned to action with a brace of goals in a 2-1 victory over Chelsea at Anfield only five days before the Hampden Park showdown with the Germans, all seemed to be well.

In fact, it wasn't. After more days of intensive treatment, which involved prolonged immersion in the icy sea at Largs, Roger was confident that his damaged joint was ready for match action. Yet on the big day, it let him down: 'I jarred it badly when I misjudged a trap from a goal-kick by Tommy Lawrence, and it swelled up at once. After that it was pretty tender.'

In the wake of the huge hype that surrounds any final, the game with Borussia materialised into a bizarre anti-climax, at least from the Liverpool viewpoint. For a start, it did not feel like a cup final. On a wet, squally night and with the game being televised live, some two-thirds of the vast, grey stadium was empty and the atmosphere matched the dreary surroundings.

Nevertheless, it was a cup final and a full-strength Reds side of Lawrence, Lawler, Byrne, Milne, Yeats, Stevenson, Callagan, Hunt, St John, Smith and Thompson had been briskly motivated, in his customary forthright manner, by Mr Shankly.

Accordingly, they pressed forward in familiar fashion and could claim to have had slightly the better of a threadbare first half in which two potentially attractive teams had cancelled each other out.

Liverpool began the second period displaying rather more spark, but went behind to a venomous volley from Sigi Held on 51 minutes. No side of Shankly's is programmed to give up, though, and back they came 17 minutes later with an equaliser which was well-deserved if controversial.

Peter Thompson danced down the flank and crossed for Roger to shoot high into the roof of Hans Tilkowski's net. The Germans protested passionately that the ball had gone over the byline before Thompson had released it - indeed, some eye-witnesses reckoned afterwards that Peter had gone behind the photographers before centering! - but with Liverpool supporters already partying on the pitch, it would have taken a brave official to rule out the goal.

Roger could offer no relevant opinion on the legality of the strike because he was in no position to see. It would be a different story over an even more hotly contested incident, involving several of these same German opponents, a couple of months later.

With parity regained, Liverpool now proceeded to grab the initiative, laying virtual siege to

The high spot of an otherwise miserable night as Roger equalises for the Reds against Borussia Dortmund in the final of the European Cup Winners' Cup at Hampden Park in May 1966. It was wet and windy, Roger was struggling with a painful ankle and Liverpool lost.

Get down . . . please! Roger gives total commitment to every game he plays and might feel he deserved a little more sympathy from fellow golfers Dennis Stevens of Everton (left) and Chester's Mike Metcalf over the fate of this putt.

the Dortmund goal, and they might have sealed victory with 60 seconds left when Roger missed an excellent opening from close range. Here, finally, he and his team paid the price for that dodgy ankle; had he been blessed with his usual mobility and confidence, the First Division's leading marksman would surely have made no mistake.

But there was worse to come. Shortly after the extra-time interval, a clearance by Lawrence rebounded to Reinhardt Libuda on Borussia's right wing. Though Tommy was off his line, Ron Yeats was in position in the six-yard box and there seemed no immediate threat.

However, Libuda saw things differently. Running full tilt, he hit the ball first time from some 35 yards and it ballooned skywards, seemingly destined to sail wildly into touch. But just as cries of relief were forming on Liverpool lips, the ball took a wicked trajectory, curving tantalisingly over Big Ron before hitting the far post and bouncing into the net off the frantically lunging skipper.

Many observers believe to this day that Libuda's effort was a freak, though Roger is convinced that it was an inspirational piece of finishing by one of Europe's top players. Whatever, it simply didn't matter; there were no more goals and the prize had slipped away.

The players were upset, as much for Shankly as themselves, because he had worked unsparingly to prepare them for Continental competition and was desperately keen to land a European trophy. His time would come, though not for another seven years.

Meanwhile Roger Hunt turned his mind to other, more pressing matters. For him, the onset of summer '66 did not signal holiday time.

COME IN NUMBER 21

Roger Hunt was a happy man to be named by Alf Ramsey in England's party of 22 players for the 1966 World Cup finals - but then his blood ran cold. When the squad numbers for the tournament were issued, Jimmy Greaves was handed number eight and Geoff Hurst received number ten; Roger, meanwhile, was left to ponder the ominous implications of being presented with number 21.

The Liverpool marksman's unease was understandable. After his first call to his country's colours in the spring of 1962, there had been only a handful of international appearances - the highlight of which had been a four-goal haul in the 10-0 thrashing of the USA in New York in 1964 - before Jimmy Greaves fell prey to jaundice in the autumn of 1965.

The Londoner's strength-sapping illness had reopened the England door for Roger, who had stepped through it with alacrity. His hard-running, honest approach had dovetailed perfectly into the Ramsey scheme of things, and he had been especially impressive in the recent seven-goal thriller against Scotland at Hampden Park, contributing two strikes to a morale-raising 4-3 victory.

Accordingly, even though Greaves was fit again, he expected to make the World Cup squad and had a right to be disappointed by the supporting role he feared was in prospect: 'I am not making the slightest criticism of Alf Ramsey, who always treated me fairly and did what he thought was right for the team. But I had done pretty well as Jimmy Greaves' deputy and, especially after the Scotland game, I half fancied I might be in the first team.'

The massive crowd at Hampden Park is hushed as Roger Hunt dispatches a goal-bound shot past Billy Bremner and 'keeper Bobby Ferguson. Roger netted twice in a pulsating encounter in which England beat Scotland 4-3 in April 1966.

However, he was certain that the players allotted shirts one to eleven were Alf's first choices at that juncture, and he was not surprised when there was no personal explanation from the manager: 'That wasn't Alf's way. He probably thought I'd be delighted just to be there.'

Fortunately for Roger, who had been undergoing intensive treatment at Lilleshall for the ankle problem that had reduced his effectiveness in the European Cup Winners' Cup final, England had a warm-up tour of Scandinavia before the tournament began. He made the most of it, while Geoff Hurst struggled to find form.

Hunt played well and scored in a 3-0 win over Finland, then retained his place for the encounter with Norway, though he didn't make the scoresheet in a 6-1 victory while Greaves notched four. He was omitted from the team which beat Denmark 2-0, but was recalled for the last game of the tour, against Poland, and responded with a fulminating 25-yard strike, the only goal of the match.

Roger recalls: 'During the tour I got back to 100-per-cent fitness and thought that I hadn't played badly. Despite my number 21, I reckoned now that I still had a chance for the finals. By that time I'd got 12 goals in 13 internationals and seemed to fit in well with the other players. All along my attitude had been that I had to keep pegging away and hope that something broke for me. I could do no more.'

There were six days between the Poland game and England's Wembley date with Uruguay, the curtain-raiser of the main event, and Ramsey let five of them pass before he put Roger out of his agony: 'I was both delighted and relieved when he told me I was in. Now all I wanted to do was get started.'

Ramsey had opted for Jimmy Greaves and Roger Hunt, with Geoff Hurst the one to make way, though all concerned were acutely aware that the selection was for only the first match. 'After that we realised that anything could happen, though I think most people felt it boiled down to who played alongside Jimmy - either Geoff or myself. The way things turned out just underlines the uncertainty of football.'

Looking back nearly 30 years after the event, it is instructive to recall that the tournament which was to end in gilded triumph for England actually began in mind-numbingly frustrating manner. The Uruguayans were an extravagantly gifted team, every player enviably comfortable on the ball, but were so hidebound by the fear of losing that they opted for purely negative tactics. England were unable to break them down and a goalless draw was the inevitable outcome.

As Roger says: 'It was a big disappointment to the public after the massive build-up, and it all served to increase the pressure for our next match, against Mexico.'

That began with similar stalemate, though Roger thought he had broken through early on when he netted with a header: 'It was disallowed, but I still don't know why. After that the crowd started getting impatient and we began to wonder if we were ever going to score.'

It was 38 minutes into an increasingly edgy encounter that England recorded their first goal of the 1966 World Cup finals. Given its context, and the power and the beauty of its execution, it remains one of the defining moments of the tournament.

The scorer was Bobby Charlton, whose spellbinding combination of silk and dynamite has rarely been more tellingly exhibited, but Roger Hunt, too, deserves a rather more significant share of the plaudits than were spared for him at the time.

Roger picked up the ball in the old left-half position, some 15 yards inside his own half, then slipped a simple, square pass to Bobby on his right. Manchester United's balding maestro carried the ball forward with that characteristic, gazelle-like grace; defenders seemed to fall away from him as he feinted left, then jinked right before unleashing one of his trademark thunderbolts from 25 yards, the ball rebounding from the stanchion while Mexican 'keeper Ignacio Calderon was still airborne.

It is fascinating to hear two of soccer's most engagingly self-effacing individuals give their versions of this milestone moment.

Roger first: 'I gave Bobby the ball and made a bit of a run. He took it on and hit the sweetest shot you could imagine. It was an example of everything that was best about Bobby, a great individual goal.'

Now Bobby: 'I would never have scored that goal without Roger Hunt. I carried the ball into their territory to see what would happen. Roger set off on a long diagonal run to my right, then darted back towards the centre, pulling the defenders in all directions. They didn't know which way to go, whether to try and stick with him or keep track of me. In the end, Roger was in the more forward position and they assumed I was likely to pass it to him, so I was able to shoot. All along, Roger knew exactly what he was doing. It was absolutely typical of his unselfish running off the ball to make things happen for his team-mates.'

After playing a noble but largely unsung part in setting up Bobby Charlton's opening goal, Roger clinched England's World Cup victory over Mexico with this comparatively simple tap-in.

Elsewhere in this book, Bobby speaks affectionately of Roger, both as friend and colleague. But for now the renowned star's generous view of the build-up to his own spectacular goal offers ample evidence that the so-called bit-part player was short-changed when it came to the subsequent praise.

Of course, back in the 1960s there were no panels of TV experts scrutinising every last piece of the action. As a result, tactics were examined only in the most cursory fashion and such subtle contributions as running to create space would have been highlighted rarely, if ever.

Should a goal such as Charlton's against Mexico be transported to a modern setting, he would still be lionised, quite rightly, for its sheer quality. But, also, perceptive pundits such as Alan Hansen and the oddly underrated Andy Gray (for this writer's money, comfortably the most illuminating of them all) would wax lyrical over Hunt's input and, during the course of countless screen replays, he would receive some of the kudos he so richly deserved.

When told of the value Bobby placed on his efforts, Roger smiles with a hint of embarrassment at such lavish appreciation from his eminent former team-mate and says: 'Running off the ball was just part of my job. I never had any coaching in that aspect of playing up front, but I suppose I had an instinct for it, how to run into space while staying onside. It was particularly important with England; I was used to playing with two wingers for Liverpool but Alf played 4-3-3, then 4-4-2. It meant more running and less of the ball for me, but I adapted.'

Near the end of the match with Mexico, Roger did garner a share of the glory when he doubled his side's lead, side-footing home from close range after Calderon had failed to hold a Greaves cross-shot.

Roger nods home the goal that finished off France at Wembley and ensured that England qualified for the quarter-finals of the 1966 World Cup. With typical modesty, he described his task as straightforward, but as the picture shows, there was still plenty to do after Ian Callaghan's cross reached his head.

Now England had lift-off, as Roger recalls: 'The belief began to flow through the side. We hadn't conceded a goal and hadn't looked like doing so. Now we were confident that we would qualify for the quarter-finals.' There was a further hurdle to be cleared, however, in the shape of France, and England's third match turned into a personal triumph for Roger as he scored both goals in a 2-0 win. Neither were of the sensational variety, but both stemmed from his knack of being in the right place at the right time.

'The first one, just before the break, came from a Jack Charlton header which bounced off a post, then rolled along the line to hit the other upright. I ran in and prodded it into the net. The second, near the end, came from a cross from Cally which I headed in from close range. I beat Martin Peters to it, either of us could have scored.'

Yet despite reaching the last eight, the game was marred for the players because Herbin had been injured in a tackle with Nobby Stiles and there was a hail of protest about so-called dirty play.

'Nobby, a nice lad, was very upset but Alf stood by him, which was typical. I didn't appreciate it at the time, but now it strikes me that every member of that team was an honest trier, irrespective of ability. It seems clear now why Alf chose the men he did and it's a tribute to his acumen and his judgement of character. He knew that, no matter what the circumstances, he could always rely on a certain level of performance.'

England's place in the quarter-finals had been attained at a cost. Greaves had suffered a gashed shin, being replaced, fatefully, by Hurst in what proved to be a momentous clash with Argentina. The South Americans, arguably the most talented team in the tournament, did themselves a grave injustice in one of the most ill-tempered displays ever witnessed on the international stage.

Roger reflects: 'We just didn't see the best of them. They were known for their spoiling tactics and play-acting, but this time they were different class, with all their hacking and spitting. I remember the full-back Marzolini, supposedly one of their nice guys, kicking me for no reason when the ball was nowhere near. That behaviour seems to be imbued in them and it's a great shame, because they could play so beautifully. Even after Rattin, their captain, was sent off, there was no way we could relax because they were always capable of creating chances.'

England won by the only goal of the game, an all-West Ham affair which had Hurst glancing home an exquisite near-post header from a Peters cross. Afterwards, Roger recalls, Ramsey was immensely pleased that his players had kept their heads in the face of severe provocation.

'He was normally an introvert with the press, preferring to keep his counsel, but he spoke out now, calling the Agentinians animals. I have never seen him so upset as he was at the end of that game. He wouldn't even allow George Cohen to swap shirts. It was a disgraceful show by the Argentinians and it soured the day.'

However, when the immediate controversy died down, the fact sank in that England were in the semi-finals. Roger looks back: 'Now we felt we were on the edge of something. The expectations of the country had grown and it was nerve-wracking. It wasn't helpful that Alf had been quoted all over the place as saying that England would win the World Cup, but in fairness to him, that came about by accident. At first I think he said merely that England COULD win. He didn't mean it to sound the way it did. But then he was stuck with it and found himself repeating it.'

Despite his goals and generally solid form to date, Roger was by no means confident of a place for the last-four clash with Portugal: 'Geoff had scored the winner against Argentina and with Jimmy's fitness being touch and go, the southern press were talking about Hunt versus Greaves - and there was no doubt where their sympathies lay. There was an endless clamour for Jimmy to play, but I had managed three goals in four games so I felt I had a realistic chance. Geoff was also a bit worried and we were both relieved to be named.'

In the event, both men excelled, complementing each other in a match which offered a glowing contrast to the infamous contest which had preceded it. As Roger points out, England had reached the semi-final in somewhat scrappy manner, what with the frustration of the Uruguay encounter, the Stiles incident against France and the Argentinian controversy: 'But the game against Portugal made up for it all. It was played in a wonderful spirit with nothing to spoil it. Both teams performed well, and Eusebio . . . he was brilliant.'

England won 2-1, with Bobby Charlton scoring two equally magnificent but vividly contrasting goals. Roger was intimately involved in the first, chasing a long ball from Ray Wilson, only for 'keeper Pereira to clear with his knees; it rebounded to Charlton who threaded it with cool precision through a crowded area, all along the ground and into the net. Once more, Bobby was grateful to his faithful provider: 'It was Roger who laid the groundwork for that one; his aggression caused the 'keeper to panic.'

The second goal was more typically Charlton, a savage blast from a Hurst set-up, which gave England the safety cushion they were to need when Portugal hit back with a late penalty.

Roger suppresses a shudder as he recalls: 'We thought we were through after Bobby's second, but Portugal came back strongly and we suffered a torrid last five minutes.' When the final whistle blew and the shirts were exchanged - no objections from Alf after such a Corinthian epic - the enormity of England's position began to sank in.

'Brazil, Italy, Hungary, Portugal, Argentina - they were all very fine sides and they were all gone,' muses Roger. 'But WE were still there, WE were in the World Cup Final! What the players wanted to know now - especially Jimmy, Geoff and myself - was who was going to play . . .'

A DIFFERENT DIMENSION

Roger Hunt was shivering in his boots. The speculation over England's team for the World Cup Final against West Germany was mounting frenziedly, though the only realistic doubts surrounded the striking positions. Jimmy Greaves was fit once more, giving Alf Ramsey three possible permutations. Would it be Hunt and Hurst? Or Greaves and Hurst? Or maybe Hunt and Greaves?

For Roger, the Wednesday and Thursday before Saturday's denouement at Wembley passed in an agony of apprehension. He can laugh about it now, but the tension at the time was well-nigh unbearable: 'For a couple of days, Alf didn't give the slightest hint. Nobody knew who would be in the side. Despite playing in all five games during the tournament so far, I wasn't convinced I'd be there.

'It kept going through my mind that Geoff had played in the last two matches and done extremely well, Jimmy was the star who could give the team an extra dimension; I could be the one to miss out, which would have been devastating after all that had happened.'

He stresses that, contrary to what many people imagined, and despite all the newspaper pressure for Jimmy Greaves to take his place in the team, he was good friends with his Tottenham counterpart. 'I must admit, though, that I got sick of the Hunt versus Greaves debate over the years, especially when we weren't vying for the same place all the time, but actually turning out alongside each other.'

Alf Ramsey has never revealed publicly whether he was taking time to make up his mind or just keeping his footballers on their toes, but he left it until the Friday before informing the players involved of their fate.

Roger remembers the day vividly: 'We were staying at the Hendon Hall Hotel and, to break up the monotony of waiting, we had gone to watch a film. It was as we were getting off the coach to go into the cinema that Alf told me I'd be playing at Wembley. It was completely unexpected at that moment and was no more than a quiet word, spoken privately.

'I couldn't think straight. I had just heard that I was going to play in the most important game in England's history. The film passed in something of a daze for me - I think it was a cowboy, probably starring John Wayne. I don't know if anyone noticed any oddness in my behaviour but the team was not being announced officially until the next morning, so I didn't feel able to tell anyone, not even my room-mate, John Connelly.

'But it was a tremendous weight off my mind. I couldn't wait to phone home and after that I didn't sleep too badly. I knew that whatever happened now, at least I would be part of it.'

When the team was announced, Greaves greeted his omission with magnanimous grace. Despite his personal elation, Roger felt desperately sorry for the perky little Londoner: 'Jimmy had been a regular for six or seven years and had scored an enormous number of goals. Now he was going to miss out on the biggest match of them all. It was absolutely terrible for him, but on the surface, at least, he seemed to take it okay. There was no animosity or grudges and he said that if anyone had to have his place then he would pick me. That was really nice of him, a lovely touch. But after the game he just disappeared. It must have hurt an awful lot.'

Roger felt sympathy, too, for the three wingers who had played in the early stages of the tournament but were then discarded in favour of the all-round contributions of Alan Ball and Martin Peters. John Connelly had played against Uruguay, Terry Paine had faced Mexico and Roger's close friend and Anfield colleague Ian Callaghan had lined up against France.

'None of them had played badly and Cally, I thought, had performed particularly well. But Alf went for the extra safety of another man in midfield. Alan Ball was such a prodigious worker, and although there were various permutations Alf could have employed, it was

One man and his marker. Throughout most of the World Cup Final, wherever Roger Hunt went, Wolfgang Weber was sure to follow.

probably Alan who took the winger's place.'

The morning of the match dawned clear and bright, and the players went for a stroll to relax before lunch. Roger was never one to be consumed by anxiety prior to an important game, but this time there were a few flutters. He recalls: 'It was such a big occasion. My greatest ambition until this point had been to play in the FA Cup Final, but this was a different dimension. In fact, I still feel a bit nervous talking about it all these years later.'

The teams on that momentous afternoon at Wembley lined up as follows.

England: Gordon Banks (Leicester City), George Cohen (Fulham), Ray Wilson (Everton), Nobby Stiles (Manchester United), Jack Charlton (Leeds United), skipper Bobby Moore (West Ham United), Alan Ball (Blackpool), Roger Hunt (Liverpool), Bobby Charlton (Manchester United), Geoff Hurst and Martin Peters (both West Ham United).

West Germany: Hans Tilkowski (Borussia Dortmund), Horst-Dieter Hottges (Werder Bremen), Karl-Heinz Schnellinger (AC Milan), Franz Beckenbauer (Bayern Munich), Willie Schulz (Hamburg), Wolfgang Weber (FC Cologne), Helmut Haller (Bologna), Wolfgang Overath (FC Cologne), skipper Uwe Seeler (Hamburg), Sigi Held and Lothar Emmerich (both Borussia Dortmund).

The game got off to a start that causes Roger to blanch at the memory: 'Usually, once you get on the field, you forget everything else. Any suggestion of nerves disappear right away and you just get on with the job. But this time, I've got to admit, the occasion got to me. For ten minutes or so the game seemed to be passing me by. Then the ball came to me, I miscontrolled it and it jolted me back to normality. I knew it was time to get a grip. My professionalism took over and I felt better.'

However, the red-shirted England side continued to look unsettled overall, and after 13 minutes an uncharacteristically edgy header from Ray Wilson allowed Haller to put the Germans in front. Thus jolted, the home team reacted in the required manner and six minutes later Hurst lost his marker to head in Moore's delightfully flighted free-kick.

Roger takes up the story: 'Even after we had equalised, I still wasn't in the game enough for my own liking for the rest of the half. The Germans were playing Schulz as a sweeper and Alf told us not to give him freedom to push the ball around as he liked. That meant extra off-the-ball work in the heat, and I was also chasing back farther than usual just to get into the action. I had just one chance in the first period, a left-footer, but I didn't get hold of it properly and Tilkowski saved. That summed up the first half for me and I thought 1-1 was a fair reflection of play.'

After the interval, though, Roger felt matters improved: 'The longer the game went on, the better I thought I was playing and the more room I was getting. I was being marked by Weber, who followed me everywhere as he had done for FC Cologne against Liverpool in the European Cup, and because I was carrying out Alf's instructions I was close to Schulz most of the time, too. But as the minutes ticked by, the markers began to tire.'

When Martin Peters volleyed England in front after 77 minutes, the World Cup hove tantalisingly within reach of Ramsey's men. Yet there remained several melodramatic twists in this particular script, even if the final minute of normal time was well advanced before they began to unfold.

It was then that the Germans were awarded a warmly disputed free-kick outside the England box. Emmerich thundered his shot into the defensive wall, then followed a pinball-style sequence which climaxed with Weber sweeping the ball into the England net. There was barely time for a re-start before the final whistle blew.

Roger relives that traumatic moment: 'I think we were all in shock, no one could believe what had happened. There was an immediate feeling of emptiness. We thought we had it won and then it was snatched away at the death. Stamina had always been one of my strongest suits, but now I felt unbelievably tired.

'Then Alf came on to the pitch and he was completely calm, which was just what we needed. He told us we had won it once, now we would have to go out and win it again. He told us we were better than the Germans and fitter than them, and I think we proved that in extra time. Certainly I felt fitter than Weber, who was giving me more and more room. The legs were weary but I found some reserves from somewhere and I think we were the stronger side throughout the extra half-hour.'

The pivotal and most controversial moment in the match, the tournament, the whole of English football history, came near the end of the first period of added time - and Roger Hunt was in the eye of the storm.

He can remember it as though it happened yesterday: 'Nobby Stiles sent Alan Ball through on the right and he cut back a pass to Geoff Hurst, who was about 10 yards out from the near post. He collected the ball cleanly, then swivelled and hit a strong, clean shot which hammered against the bar and bounced down.

'I was running in, sniffing for rebounds, and was about six yards out when the ball hit the ground. I saw the ball cross the line and I turned instantly to celebrate the goal. I believed at the time that it was over the line and I believe it now. If there had been the slightest shred of doubt in my mind I'd have followed it in to make sure.

'Then I looked back to my left and Weber had headed the ball away. Some of the Germans were appealing to the referee and suddenly I had visions of the goal being disallowed. The linesman was not up with play, not really in a position to see what happened, but the referee went to discuss the incident with him. They were surrounded by German players

and Ball and I went with them. Then the linesman gave the goal (in effect) and there was a fantastic eruption of noise.

'I have seen so much film since and none of it is conclusive, but I am still convinced I was right at the time. I sympathise with the officials, though. It was an incredibly difficult decision, which had to be given instantly with the eyes of the world on them.'

At 3-2 Roger recalls feeling fabulous, but still a trifle wary because he knew that the Germans would never give up. Quite simply, surrender just wasn't in their make-up. The game became increasingly ragged and as the end neared all semblance of defensive covering disappeared. Then Bobby Moore hit a long ball to Hurst who, in an almost surreal atmosphere, struck the final blow. The score was 4-2 and it was all over.

Roger again: 'When the last whistle blew I felt ten feet tall. It was incredible. At first it wouldn't sink in that we were champions of the world. A little later the joy was followed by a vast sense of relief that it was all over. There had been so much strain and expectation, all tied up with not knowing whether I was going to play.

'It was absolute chaos on the pitch, both before and after the presentation. Alf just sat there poker-faced in the midst of it all. He wouldn't run around with the cup, he left that to the players. He just went round to each of us individually and thanked us for our efforts. Not effusively, but it was obviously from the heart. He must have felt wonderful inside - after all, he'd proved the world and all his critics wrong - but he wouldn't let it show. Somehow it was as though it wouldn't have been properly English to do that.'

It wasn't until much later, at his leisure, that Roger began to reflect on the scale of the achievement and his own place in the history books. That niche was secure, and though the knockers who had battered him throughout his England career didn't lay down their cudgels even now, they could never take that away from him.

Was it over the line? This photograph, like every other picture of the most controversial goal in the history of English football, fails to provide conclusive proof. Suffice it to say that Roger Hunt (dark shirt, nearest the ball) was utterly convinced. He declares: 'It was a goal' and the record books agree with him.

'England WILL win the World Cup,' predicted Alf Ramsey, and so they did. Here are the newly crowned world champions on that never-to-be-forgotten Wembley afternoon in July 1966. Left to right, back row: trainer Harold Shepherdson, Jack Charlton, Gordon Banks, Roger Hunt, skipper Bobby Moore waving the Jules Rimet trophy, Geoff Hurst, George Cohen and Bobby Charlton. Front row: Nobby Stiles, Alan Ball, Martin Peters and Ray Wilson.

AFTER THE LORD MAYOR'S SHOW

If Roger Hunt had expected his part in England's World Cup triumph to usher in a new era of sweetness and light as far as the national press were concerned, he was to be sorely mistaken.

Come the autumn, after an early gush of club goals had dried up and with Jimmy Greaves (that man again) scoring freely for Spurs, the old cry went up on the back pages. Sure enough, the southern-based scribes reckoned Roger was tired from his World Cup exertions and that it was time for a change.

Deep down he wasn't phased by the carping, although there were times when he found it irritating. He explains: 'Because of the system that Alf played, I didn't stand out for England in the way that I did for Liverpool. His 4-4-2 meant lots of hard, off-the-ball running for me and many people didn't realise what was involved. It was foreign to what I was used to and the critics didn't understand or make allowances for that.'

Indeed over several seasons the London papers never stopped calling for Jimmy Greaves. Roger was never popular with them, no matter what he did. The most he would get in the reports would be 'hard working'. It would never be 'brilliant', even when he had scored from 25 yards.

One consolation, though, was that Alf Ramsey never paid any attention to such ignorant prejudice, though there was an occasion when he left Roger out in apparent agreement with a press campaign.

It was the fourth international after the World Cup, against Scotland at Wembley, and even more than usual was at stake in this meeting of the 'auld enemies'. Not only was the

Left: When Liverpool met Everton in the 1966 Charity Shield, the four Merseyside-based members of England's World Cup party were honoured with special gifts to mark their achievement. Left to right are Gerry Byrne, lone Evertonian Ray Wilson, Ian Callaghan and Roger Hunt.

Opposite: Roger Hunt and Ray Wilson parade around Goodison Park with the most prestigious prize of all.

now-defunct Home Championship at stake, the game also counted towards qualification for the European Nations Cup finals - and then there was the little matter of the Scots' passionate desire to put one over on the world champions.

Since lifting the trophy, England had beaten Northern Ireland 2-0 (with Hunt scoring once), been held to a goalless draw by Czechoslovakia, and brushed aside Wales 5-1. However, at club level, Roger had been below par.

He grins philosophically as he reflects: 'Alf left me out against Scotland. I suppose I shouldn't have been surprised to be the first member of the team that beat West Germany to be dropped, particularly as I hadn't been doing so well for Liverpool. But Alf didn't often go on club form, preferring to back his own knowledge and long-term judgement, so it was a bit puzzling.

'As it turned out we lost to Scotland and after the match he came up to me and said: "I don't suppose you're speaking to me." Of course, that wasn't the case and he took me to one side and apologised, saying he had been wrong to leave me out. That was good of him, he didn't have to do it.'

Roger was restored to the side for the next match, a friendly with Spain at Wembley, and duly scored in a 2-0 victory. But a slow change had been taking place in his private attitude to international football: 'After the World Cup I was 28 years old and I considered that I was at my peak. But at the back of my mind, although it was still a tremendous honour to play for my country and I wanted to continue, I couldn't see myself going on to another World Cup.

'By then I would be 32 and I didn't have the burning ambition to go through it all again. My role in the 4-4-2 system was taxing and I didn't really relish it. It offered valuable experience but was very hard to fulfil, both mentally and physically.'

However, he was not ready to throw in the international towel, playing on through and past the European Championships of 1968, turning in some of his most effective displays. Nevertheless, it is significant that after scoring 15 times in his first 16 England appearances, there were only three more goals in his remaining 18 outings, more a reflection on evolving team tactics than any diminution of powers.

After his omission against Scotland, Roger enjoyed a five-match sequence back in favour before being dropped once more in February 1968, again when the Scots were the opponents. Then he was back in for the two-legged European Championship quarter-final against Spain - England won 3-1 on aggregate - and scored his final international goal in a Wembley friendly against Sweden in May 1968.

Roger's last big occasion in an England shirt came two weeks later in the Stadio Communale in Florence, where Ramsey's gradually changing side - Keith Newton, Alan Mullery, Brian Labone and Norman Hunter were all on duty - faced Yugoslavia in the European Championship semi-final.

Sadly, it was a sour encounter, with the Slavs allying physical chicanery to their undoubted natural talent, and on a humid night it was not surprising that tempers frayed. What did raise a few eyebrows, though, was that one of the men to see red was Roger Hunt, who became involved in an unseemly scuffle after being fouled for the umpteenth time.

Luckily, Bobby Charlton, ever the peacemaker, was on hand to defuse the situation; less happily, Dzajic netted the only goal of the game with four minutes left and Mullery became the first England man to be sent off in a full international when he retaliated following dire provocation.

No one knew it at the time, but Roger's days in an England shirt were drawing to a close. After helping to overcome Russia to claim third place in the European Championships, then playing in two frustratingly barren friendlies with Rumania, he informed his manager that he was ready to retire from international football.

Some felt it was a rash step, but the Hunt mind was not for changing: 'Alf said to me "You mean you're not coming with me to Mexico for the World Cup?" but he accepted my decision graciously and thanked me for all my efforts in the past. There was no extravagant reaction. He didn't show any emotion and I wouldn't have expected any. That was never the nature of the man.'

Did Roger feel any subsequent regret that he walked away from the white shirt which was coveted by so many, yet offered to so few?

'I must admit, when I saw the lads leaving for Mexico I did feel a few slight misgivings, particularly with my clubmate Emlyn Hughes making the trip. But it was only a fleeting feeling.'

He believed, along with many contemporary observers, that Ramsey's class of '70 was superior in many ways to the '66 combination and that they set off with a realistic chance of retaining the world title.

'Alf had had more time to perfect his system and the team was probably better balanced by the time Mexico came around. People forget that there was plenty of last-minute tinkering in '66.'

Nevertheless, it is the '66 campaign, in which Roger played such an integral part, which will retain forever a revered place in English soccer folklore. His international career was over, but at least he had scaled the ultimate pinnacle.

With an England record encompassing 34 caps and 18 goals, 25 victories and only two defeats, not to mention a small but priceless gold medal, Roger Hunt could be a satisfied man.

And, if his natural modesty would allow it, a proud one, too.

Northern Ireland 'keeper Pat Jennings fears the worst, but Roger is not about to score for England at Windsor Park, Belfast, in October 1966. He did manage to find the net during the game, however, and the visitors won 2-0.

A MOMENTOUS MILESTONE

After the World Cup, Roger Hunt felt good. Not tired or jaded as the snipers suggested later; just very, very good. And why not? He was revelling in his new-found freedom from the strain engendered by England's expectations, and his early performances boded well for the taxing tests - including his second European Cup campaign - that were beckoning.

He scored the only goal in the Charity Shield triumph against Everton and just ten minutes into the League season he netted to set Liverpool on the way to a home victory over Leicester. There followed a brace of Hunt strikes in a 3-2 Anfield victory over Manchester City, and although there had been two away defeats in between, the Merseysiders had often been slow starters so there was no apparent cause for concern.

However, come late autumn and early winter, it was clear that all was not as it should be. Roger's well of goals was running dry and the most frustrating aspect of the drought was that there was no obvious cause.

'My ankle was perfectly okay by now, but I just wasn't scoring. For the first time since I had signed for Liverpool I was having a lean spell, which comes to every striker at some time in his career. Bill Shankly's philosophy was just to keep on playing and it would come right in the end. I don't think I was ever in danger of being dropped by Liverpool, though I was left out by England against Scotland. It was all very worrying.'

The Reds' European travail did not help matters. After struggling through the preliminary round in a replay against the unfancied but doggedly tenacious Rumanians, Petrolul Ploesti, Liverpool were utterly outclassed by an emerging Ajax side in which a young man named Johan Cruyff took the breath away.

Recalls Roger: 'Little was known about Ajax in those days, though they were soon to rule Europe. They were a far better side than we imagined, as they proved by beating us 5-1 in Amsterdam. Cruyff was absolutely marvellous, obviously a world star in the making. Yet even with a four-goal deficit, Shanks gave us belief that we might get back in it at Anfield.'

It didn't turn out that way, the 2-2 draw dumping Liverpool out of Europe, and when an Alan Ball goal at Goodison Park unseated them from the FA Cup and a late-season League slump saw the title slip away to Old Trafford, it added up to the club's first major letdown since gaining promotion.

Of course, both the Reds' and Roger's so-called declines should be kept in proportion. The club finished fifth in the First Division, nine points behind the champions, and their main marksman managed 18 goals in all senior competitions - hardly disastrous.

However, Shankly knew that radical action was necessary and wasted no time in taking it. Out went wing-halves Gordon Milne and Willie Stevenson, skilful operators both but whose input had arguably lost a little zest, and into a restructured midfield, in which St John dropped ever deeper, came Emlyn Hughes, who was not nicknamed 'Crazy Horse' for being a shrinking violet.

Meanwhile Tony Hateley, an 'old-fashioned' dreadnought of a centre-forward, arrived from Chelsea to form with Roger a double spearhead of formidable potential. Thus the 'H-Bombers' were born and soon they were living up to the hype, Roger scoring both goals in a morale-boosting home win over Arsenal, then Tony grabbing three and Roger two more in a 6-0 Anfield steamrollering of Newcastle United.

Liverpool were beginning to look awesome again and the Hunt hiccup of 1966/67 seemed a distant memory. In fact, it was to be a magnificent personal term for Roger, though the team was to fall fractionally short of Shankly's rigorous requirements.

Playing alongside Tony Hateley suited Roger ideally: 'Tony was brilliant in the air and scored his share, but also made many for me by nodding the ball down. The upshot was,

Opposite above: Tricky stuff from Roger as he is tackled by Everton's Colin Harvey during the 1966 Charity Shield clash at Goodison Park. Brian Labone, the Toffeemen's stopper, looks on admiringly, while referee Jack Taylor indulges in a touch of flamboyance.

Opposite below: Roger hits the target against Leicester at Anfield on the opening day of 1966/67 with grounded England colleague Gordon Banks unable to intervene. Graham Cross is the City player on the left.

Above: A spectacular salmon leap from Roger produces a goal against Stoke City at Anfield in March 1967. The Potters' defenders are Alan Bloor (left) and Tony Allen.

Right: Over they go. Roger and Tommy Lawrence, one of his best friends at Anfield, topple a pile of pennies for charity. Liverpool players were frequently called upon to help with good causes and they obliged whenever possible.

though, that the side had to change their style of play to a certain extent, relying more on long balls into the box instead of the pass-and-support game we had developed over the years. Both Willie and Gordon were excellent passers and, for a while, their influence was missed.'

For a club who had become accustomed to replenishing their trophy cabinet on a regular basis, however, it was another unfulfilling campaign. The Reds finished three points adrift of League champions Manchester City, lost a twice-replayed FA Cup quarter-final to West Bromwich Albion (who went on to beat Everton at Wembley), and bowed out in the third round of the European Fairs Cup to Ferencvaros of Hungary.

In March a header at Hillsborough had taken Roger past Billy Liddell's post-war club record of 216 League goals and he finished the season with 30 strikes in 57 senior outings, the perfect reply to those vociferous doubters who had reckoned he was past his best.

However Roger, who celebrated his 30th birthday that summer, was never to score as heavily again and 1968/69 was to mark an unwelcome watershed in his hitherto idyllic relationship with Bill Shankly.

In fact, it was a season in which Liverpool could count themselves as unfortunate not to finish as League champions. In most years, their handsome total of 61 points would have been enough to ensure that the title pennant fluttered over Anfield, but this time they ran into outstanding opposition in the form of Don Revie's Leeds United, who out-stripped the Reds by six clear points.

For Roger, it was a bitty campaign, in which his endlessly publicised efforts to beat Gordon Hodgson's all-time club scoring record loomed distractingly. After the 'H-Bombers' had managed only two goals between them in the first month or so of action, Shankly attempted to boost the strike-rate by making Wolves' Alun Evans British football's first £100,000 teenager.

Hateley was dispatched to Coventry while the feisty newcomer slotted in alongside Roger, who recalls: 'He was a lovely lad, very young and still learning but full of guts and very skilful. After he played well and scored twice when we beat Wolves 6-0 at Molineux, we all thought he was going to be a world-beater. But he suffered injuries and was hurt in a nightclub incident and, somehow, it never happened for him.'

Roger shows he can make a tackle as well as take one. On the receiving end at Upton Park in April 1968 is Ronnie Boyce of West Ham United, while Geoff Hurst awaits the outcome.

After netting only once in the first ten First Division games, Roger grabbed four in two autumn outings and suddenly all the talk was of passing Hodgson's 232 League goals, a total completed in 1935/36.

The would-be record-breaker looks back somewhat ruefully: 'I wasn't scoring many at all and, for some reason, I wasn't getting ANY at home. I felt I wasn't playing too badly but I grew extremely frustrated. The longer this record was in the offing the worse it got. I became very anxious and didn't seem to have a scrap of luck - goalkeepers seemed to reserve their best saves for me, I would hit the woodwork repeatedly, there seemed to be nothing I could do.

'Finally I equalled the record at Nottingham Forest on November 30, and dearly wanted to break it at Anfield, but it just wouldn't happen. In fact, it was another six weeks before I man-

Above: Roger the record-breaker. The Reds' spearhead beats Ron 'Chopper' Harris and 'keeper Tommy Hughes to score against Chelsea at Stamford Bridge in January 1969, thus breaking Gordon Hodgson's Liverpool record of 232 League goals and ending weeks of frustration.

Below: Contrasting emotions. Ian Callaghan and Alun Evans (right) rush to congratulate Roger on reaching the milestone, while Chelsea's Peter Osgood (left) and John Hollins protest that the goal should be ruled out.

aged it, at Chelsea. The fans had been terrifically supportive - the Kop seemed to be trying to suck the ball in for me - but I feel I stretched their patience to the limit and it was a tremendous relief when the waiting was over.'

Amid all the tension, it was easy to emphasise the sense of release without dwelling sufficiently on the scale of Roger's achievement. It was, of course, immense, not least because his total of 233 League goals to that date had been achieved with the aid of only one penalty.

He grins: 'I only ever took two for Liverpool. One in the First Division against Burnley, which I scored, and another against Arsenal in an FA Cup tie, which Jim Furnell saved. Shanks didn't like the way I took penalties, though he thought he was pretty good himself! Most days towards the end of training he would tell Tommy Lawrence that he would score six out of six. He took ages, but he always managed it, counting any saves Tommy might make as illegal. We'd all be waiting to get changed, but that didn't matter to Shanks.'

Roger speaks of his late, great manager with a warmth which is patently sincere, yet just six weeks after he had become the leading scorer in Liverpool's history, the two men were to clash, suddenly and bitterly, and relations between them would come under considerable strain.

Another day, another record: Roger propels a powerful header past Sheffield Wednesday goalkeeper Peter Springett at Hillsborough in March 1968 to replace Billy Liddell as Liverpool's leading post-war League goal-scorer. Unable to prevent him are Wednesday defenders Peter Eustace (left) and Wilf Smith.

THE LEAVING OF LIVERPOOL

What would previously have been deemed unthinkable, a blazing row with the figurehead and founder of the modern Reds, was sparked by Shanks' decision to substitute Roger during an FA Cup fourth-round replay with Leicester City at Anfield. The first game at Filbert Street had ended goalless; now, about midway through the second half of the rematch and with Liverpool trailing 1-0, Bobby Graham was sent on to replace the England striker.

What followed should be taken in the context that in Roger's ten years at Anfield, he had never been dropped or substituted, and there had never been the slightest suggestion that he might be. It must be remembered, also, that allowing tactical substitutions was a relatively new innovation and there had never been any discussions at the club about football now being a 12-man game.

Thus it was against such a background that Roger was amazed to see Bobby running up and down the track, apparently preparing to come on. Still perplexed by the memory, Roger takes up the story: 'Even then it didn't dawn on me that I was to be replaced until Ron Yeats approached me and said he thought the management wanted me off. I said words to the effect that they could get stuffed and Ron left it at that. We went on playing but there was increasing commotion on the touchline. Then the referee came to me and said I was being called off.

'I had no choice then, but as I passed the bench, in front of more than 54,000 fans, I pulled off my shirt and threw it into the dugout before marching straight inside to have a bath. It was out of character, perhaps ill-advised, but I was angry, frustrated and puzzled by what had happened.'

In the dressing-room after the 1-0 defeat, Bill Shankly and Roger Hunt exchanged heated words: 'He said he'd thought I was a sportsman; I said I didn't think I'd deserved to be treated like that. It was very quiet around us as we spoke. I don't think anyone could credit what was going on and there was enormous disappointment with the result, especially as we were already out of the Fairs Cup (on the toss of a coin, to Atletico Bilbao).'

Tommy Smith remembers the shirt-throwing episode vividly: 'It stands out as the only time I ever saw Roger show dissent. I suppose Shanks was thinking more about the club than the player, but he might have been more diplomatic about it. I can well understand the way Roger felt.'

Later, when passions had cooled, Roger remained disturbed by what had taken place: 'It seemed that Bill Shankly had lost faith in me after my ten years at the club and it came as a big shock. I wondered if this was the thin end of the wedge and thought I might be on the way out. Of course, most people wouldn't think twice if they were substituted in modern football, but things were different then. It wasn't just me - the lads couldn't believe what had happened.

'I was back in for the next game but my confidence had been damaged. I hadn't been playing particularly well but felt I was always liable to get a goal. I don't think Bob Paisley and the others were happy with what had gone on, but Shanks was the boss and it was up to him to do what he thought was best for Liverpool. I must stress too, that after all we had gone through together there was no way we were going to lose the tremendous respect and affection we held for each other. Anyway, he continued to pick me but I couldn't shake off the feeling that the writing was on the wall.'

The following summer, Roger turned 31 but worked harder than ever before to prepare for a new season: 'It was an echo of the way I'd worked when I arrived at the club. Once again I was determined that if I didn't succeed, it wouldn't be for the lack of effort. There were articles in the press, with Shanks saying he wanted the OLD Roger Hunt or he would have to look for something else. It was a big, big challenge for me. Fair enough, he had to strengthen the team, I accept that. But I had something to prove.'

Roger set about doing that in the only way he knew how and was involved in some sparkling team performances as the Reds got off to a nine-game unbeaten start in the League. He recalls the home encounter with Manchester City as especially enthralling, with Lee, Bell, Summerbee and company 2-1 up with just seven minutes left, only for goals from the old firm of Hunt and St John to secure the points.

Yet in the midst of this sequence, Roger was dismayed to hear from Shanks that Second Division Middlesbrough had inquired about him - and were told he might be available. Once more he felt the ground shifting beneath his feet: 'When you hear your manager say that, then you know your situation is extremely uncertain.'

Soon after that, there was another unsettling experience at Vicarage Road, shortly before a League Cup meeting with Watford. Roger recounts it as though he still struggles to believe it: 'In those days you never knew you were playing until an hour before the kick-off. There used to be a lot of ribbing from the lads if anyone got stripped and then found out they weren't picked. So unless you were an absolute certainty, you used to glance nervously at where your place in the dressing-room should be to see if your boots were there before you started to get changed.

'I had had a peek at Watford and still wasn't sure, when Bill Shankly confronted me in the corridor outside the dressing-room and asked me for a quick word. In fact, we went into the office of Ken Furphy, the Watford manager, and tipped him out - and this was only 45 minutes before the game!

'Shanks asked me how I thought I was playing. I decided not to make it easy for him and said I thought I was playing well. He said the directors didn't think so and I questioned how long he'd been taking football orders from directors.

'"Are you telling me that Bill Shankly doesn't pick his own team?" I asked. He got annoyed and said "Right, you're playing. We'll leave it as it is." I did play and we won 2-1, but that chat before the game certainly wasn't much of a confidence-builder.'

Later that September, Roger was deployed in a deep-lying role at home to Stoke City. He performed effectively, scoring the opening goal in a 3-1 victory, and Middlesbrough boss Stan Anderson - an old pal of Roger's who had made his England debut on the same day - revealed later that Shanks had gone back on his willingness to sell after that display.

At the time, understandably and correctly, Roger continued to feel insecure: 'I felt I was back to my best but didn't know where I stood. In the ten previous years there must have been offers for me, but they had never been allowed to reach my ears. Now the policy was completely different and I wondered why.'

Preparing for action, the Kopites' amiable and unassuming idol-next-door.

It was not long before he found out. Soon Roger was dropped once more and Shanks informed him that Blackburn Rovers, Blackpool and Bolton Wanderers were all keen to sign him.

'I had 18 months left on my contract, which would take me to the age of 33. To be fair, Bill said that I didn't have to go, reminded me that I had a testimonial in the offing and pointed out that the club rule was that you had to retire after that. He told me he felt Bobby Graham was playing well and indicated that he wanted to change the team a bit.

'My first thought was that I didn't want to go and that I should stay and fight for my place. At the time we were second in the League, having made our best start for years, and I had scored a few goals. But it was clear his mind was made up about the changes, and my mind went back to the game against Leicester and that shirt-throwing incident. I still had the feeling that that had spelt the beginning of the end of my Liverpool career.'

There followed several trips to away matches without even making the substitute's bench. There were also a couple of outings for the reserves and a reminder that other clubs had been given permission to contact him.

'Yet despite all that I was undecided, so I asked Gordon Milne - by then at Blackpool - for his opinion and he advised me to go. He explained that my age was against me, and the longer I left it the harder I would find it to get fixed up elsewhere.

'He thought it was better to leave while there was a chance of a few years of regular first-team football somewhere else, whereas if I hung on at Liverpool I'd probably get no more than the odd game. All my memories at Anfield were good, so why ruin it now, especially as Shanks was breaking up the team anyway.'

Gordon's well-considered thoughts made sense to his troubled former colleague and thus the die was cast. Roger Hunt decided to part company with Liverpool and a generation of Kopites - the likes of Stan Green and his mates - were left to shake their heads in dismay and disbelief.

Heroes together: Roger arrives at Burnden Park to be greeted by his boyhood favourite, the one and only Nat Lofthouse.

BOLTON - AND BEYOND

When the unthinkable occurred, and Roger Hunt bade his reluctant farewell to Liverpool, it was fitting that Bolton Wanderers should be his next and only other club. He had enjoyed a lifetime love affair with the Trotters, supporting them as an impressionable youngster through their post-war heyday, and now he would be managed by his boyhood idol, Nat Lofthouse.

Another attraction of his £32,000 transfer to Burnden Park in December 1969 was that the Hunts could remain in the family home at Culcheth, but there was no suggestion that Roger was opting for a cushy life. Bolton were a club of proud tradition, unhappy to be struggling in the wrong half of the Second Division, and were optimistic that their illustrious purchase would prove the catalyst to bring about a change of fortune.

Roger made his debut in a morale-boosting away victory against Lancashire rivals Preston North End on Boxing Day, but there was to be no easy transition from the Anfield big time to the hard realities of soccer at a lower level.

He recalls: 'During my first few weeks I would have given anything to go back to Liverpool. I knew in my heart that the time was right to leave, but I under-estimated what a massive wrench it would be. Going in to work at Anfield was like going from one home to another and I missed everything about it. I wasn't quite prepared for the change in routine.

'At Bolton, where I had signed a two-and-a-half-year contract, everything was on a smaller scale and, without being unduly critical, it was not as professional.'

Roger retains a warm personal regard for Lofthouse but was not alone in thinking that Nat was out of his depth at the time: 'He was a really nice bloke and was smashing to me, but I think he'd be the first to admit that he didn't enjoy being a manager. Bolton had not done too well in the first half of the season and he was under a lot of pressure.

'Yet still they played attacking football, with two wingers - Terry Wharton and Gordon Taylor (destined to become leader of the Professional Footballers Association) - and I thought that would suit me.'

However, Roger took time to adjust and it was not until February and his sixth game, a 2-1 home victory over Middlesbrough, that he registered his first goal for his new employers. Soon he struck up a promising link with the clever and underrated John Byrom, and with classy team-mates such as midfielder Roy Greaves and stopper Charlie Hurley there seemed every reason for believing Wanderers could climb the table.

Sadly, it never happened and Bolton finished a rather sorry 16th in the Second Division,

He became better known as a manager, but Ron Atkinson was a fair footballer in his time, too. Here Roger Hunt, on Second Division duty for Bolton Wanderers, lunges for the ball but Big Ron, the Oxford United skipper, is not giving it away lightly.

with Roger scoring five times in 18 League and Cup appearances. But if 1969/70 represented under-achievement, then 1970/71 was to bring far worse.

The season began promisingly with two victories, Roger scoring the decisive goal in the second of them, at home to Sheffield Wednesday. But then a grim decline set in against a background of increasing financial difficulty. After presiding over only three more wins, Lofthouse moved 'upstairs' to become general manager in November, leaving the coach, former Burnley and Northern Ireland play-maker Jimmy McIlroy, to assume control of team affairs.

But the new boss quickly found himself at loggerheads with the board, who wanted to sell players to raise cash, and he departed after a mere 18 days, which meant the faithful Nat had to resume the reins of a club in direst turmoil.

If ever a man needed an instant boost, it was Lofthouse, and Roger provided it the following day, hitting a second-half hat-trick which crushed Birmingham City at Burnden.

But it was only one isolated defiant gesture, and Roger reflects: 'It was a very unhappy time. I wasn't satisfied with my fitness - I kept pulling hamstrings - and the team was not playing well.'

In mid January the directors made one last attempt to avert relegation to the Third Division for the first time in the club's history by appointing Blackpool coach Jimmy Meadows as manager. Eleven weeks and only one victory later, he departed in disillusionment, and responsibility reverted to Nat Lofthouse yet again.

Such roller-coaster turbulence could have only one outcome, of course, and the tempest-tossed Trotters finished at the foot of the table. Roger, who had striven ceaselessly and never given less than his best throughout the miserable campaign, had contributed eight goals in 24 League outings (including two as substitute) but at its end, not surprisingly, he was feeling jaded.

He needed a lift and it came in the form of a summer in South Africa, playing for former England colleague George Eastham's Hellenic FC, based in Cape Town.

'I had a great time out there in the sunshine. The agreement was originally for six weeks, but things went so well that I stayed for three months and the family came out to join me. We had a smashing side - including George himself, Ian St John, Willie Stevenson, Gordon Banks, Calvin Palmer (once of Nottingham Forest and Stoke City, then with Crewe Alexandra), Ronnie Wilson (Port Vale) and Willie Hunter (Motherwell) - and we won a major trophy. Indeed, the overall standard of competition was extremely high, with other clubs

Roger Hunt relished his sojourn in South Africa, playing for an Hellenic side which contained many players who had forged respected reputations elsewhere. Left to right, back row: Roger, Calvin Palmer, Andy Rogers, Ken Allen, Tony Lupton, Peter Rath, Willie Stevenson. Front row: Willie Hunter, Ian St John, George Eastham, Wally Gould, Ron Wilson and S do Santos. This was the line-up for a 2-2 draw against Cape Town in May 1971, a match played in front of 40,000 fans.

employing the likes of Johnny Haynes, Johnny Byrne, Peter Lorimer, Johny Giles and Francis Lee.'

After that, Roger returned to Burnden Park raring to go for 1971/72, all set for the formidable challenge of attempting to bounce straight back into the Second Division. By then Jimmy Armfield, another one-time England team-mate, was the new Bolton boss and he succeeded in halting what had become an alarming downward spiral.

Roger remains reasonably content with what was to prove his final term as a professional footballer: 'I was left out a few times in the autumn but finished up starting 33 League games and scoring 11 goals, and remained mercifully free of injury.

'Part of the way through the season, several clubs, including Tranmere Rovers, inquired about taking me on loan, and Crewe Alexandra wanted me as player-boss. Jimmy Armfield gave me a similar chat to the one I'd had with Shanks, more or less telling me that he was building a new team and that soon I would be surplus to his requirements.

'I said I didn't want to play for another club, but still wanted to be in the first team at Bolton. But when he spelled out the position, fairly and clearly, I decided I would pack it in at the end of the season. I then found myself in the team for the remainder of the matches and enjoyed it, scoring quite a few goals. It was as though a load had been lifted from my shoulders and my only regret was that we couldn't win promotion. In the end we finished seventh.'

During that run of improved form, Armfield revised his thinking and offered another contract, but by then Roger had decided to have his testimonial in April 1972 and Liverpool's rule precluded playing on after that.

'There was also an awareness that once you announce your retirement date, as I had, you were setting yourself up for a possible flop if you came back, so I stuck to my guns. Yet I was still fit and I knew I could have played on. For at least a couple of years, when I was driving a lorry, as I did from time to time, I would ask myself "Why am I doing this when I could still be playing football?"

'But I took part in a lot of charity games and for the next ten years there were international tours, playing alongside people like Bobby Charlton, John Charles, Jim Baxter and Bryan Douglas. That all helped me to come to terms, gradually, with a different way of life.'

The testimonial match, between Liverpool's FA Cup-winning side of 1965 and an England X1 at Anfield, had been a deeply emotional, sensationally successful occasion, the memory of

Talent unlimited. After retiring from the professional game, Roger continued to play in charity matches alongside some of the most illustrious figures of his day. Left to right are Bertie Auld, George Cohen, Gordon Banks, Billy McNeill, Bobby Charlton, Jim Baxter and Roger.

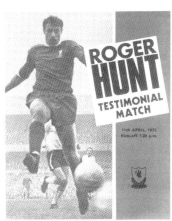

which he will always cherish.

'It was a horribly wet night and on my way to the ground I thought the weather would be certain to hit the attendance. But when I got there at 6.30 there were already about 32,000 people inside and within half an hour the gates had been closed on 56,000, with thousands more locked out.

'I was amazed and unbelievably moved. It was a marvellous tribute. I had left the club more than two years earlier and it choked me up to think the fans still felt so strongly about me. It occurred to me again that if I made any sort of comeback it could only spoil things.'

The game itself was a light-hearted exhibition, with the crowd glorying in the return of such old favourites as Milne and Stevenson and jokingly booing new hero Kevin Keegan every time he got the ball.

Roger continues: 'I walked around the pitch before the game and Shanks came to the Kop end with me. It was a supremely affecting moment as they sang *You'll Never Walk Alone*. Shanks and I had had our differences of opinion, but there would always be a bond between us. He had sent me a good-luck telegram when I played my first game for Bolton and, as we stood in front of those fantastic fans, he told me such a turnout would never happen again.

'In football, as in life, you have to move on. Nothing lasts forever. Shanks went on to build another fine team, which was to prove yet again what a great manager he was.'

After leaving Bolton in May 1972, Roger didn't even consider life as a soccer boss, not fancying the inevitable pressures and anxieties that go with the territory. Instead he thought of starting a travel agency, but then he returned to the family haulage business in which he had worked as a teenager. He played an active part for the next 23 years, before retiring in the spring of 1995.

Now divorced, and with his children grown up - David is in the freight business in Lancashire, while Julie is a journalist with the magazine *Take A Break* in London - Roger is able to find plenty of time for golf, his chief sporting passion outside football.

Night of nights: The star-spangled cast for Sir Roger's testimonial gather in the Anfield dressing room. Back row left to right: Keegan, Callaghan, Lawler, Smith, Kendall, Milne, Byrne, St John, Banks and Paisley. Middle row: Hurst, Armfield, Moore, Peters, Cohen, Yeats, Lawrence, Waiters, Stevenson (almost hidden) and Strong. Front: Stiles, Tony Brown, Roger, Shanks, Astle, Thompson and Eastham.

'I played a fair bit during my time at Liverpool, but football dominated everything at the time and I couldn't commit myself to competitive golf until I left Bolton.' Now he operates off a handicap of nine at the Leigh club, where old chum Tommy Lawrence was also once a member.

Meanwhile, he retains a connection with the game he graced for so long by continuing to serve on the Pools Panel, which he joined in 1974 and which he now chairs.

Not one for dwelling on the past, nevertheless Roger is not averse to an occasional session of poring over his extensive collection of cuttings and photographs.

'It makes me realise how fortunate I have been to be associated with so many wonderful people in the game. At Liverpool there was Shanks – who was incomparable, of course, both as a man and as a manager – as well as Bob Paisley, Joe Fagan, Reuben Bennett and some truly marvellous team mates.

'It was much the same at Bolton, where I was so well treated by Nat Lofthouse and the trainers,Eddie Hopkinson and Bert Sproston, and enjoyed once more being part of a great bunch of lads.

'Similarly it was a privilege to be involved with England under Walter Winterbottom and then Alf Ramsey, both lovely men in their contrasting ways, and trainers Harold Shepherdson and Les Cocker, both sadly no longer with us.'

'My international team-mates were magnificent, too, both on and off the field. Yes, I have been a lucky man.'

Come the autumn of '95 and Roger Hunt, an enviably fit 57-year-old who could easily pass for ten years younger, was unsure exactly what the future held.

For sure, golf would continue to be prominent on the agenda and he was contemplating promotional work. But one thing was certain. As long as football is played on Merseyside, the man they call Sir Roger will remain one of its favourite sons.

The Hunt brothers, Roger and Peter (right) like nothing better than a game of golf. Pictured with them are two like-minded friends Dave Screeton and the late Ted Cooper

FROM THE HEART

Four men who know Roger Hunt better than most, men with whom he has worked and played at the highest club and international level, share their reflections on a staunch friend and model team-mate.

TOMMY SMITH of Liverpool and England

'He was christened Sir Roger after the 1966 World Cup. When Alf Ramsey was knighted the Liverpool players decided Roger deserved a knighthood, too - or at least the Merseyside equivalent. Then the fans got to hear about it and it stuck. It was all said light-heartedly but it was not just a joke. It was impossible to exaggerate the esteem in which the lads held Roger Hunt. He was what Liverpool were all about. He played such a massive part in the resurgence of the club under Bill Shankly.

'Some people said he wasn't as good as Jimmy Greaves but I thought he was better. True, Greaves could put the ball in the net, but other than that he was lazy. Roger worked from the first minute to the last. He had more appetite for the game as a whole than Greaves.

'Roger could and often did score from any angle, from 30 yards or from two yards, but he created many more goals for his team-mates by his unselfish running, pulling defenders out of position.

'People talk about Keegan and Toshack or Rush and Dalglish when they are asked about great Liverpool striking duos, but I talk about Hunt and St John. When I pick my greatest ever Liverpool team - as I am requested to do from time to time - then Roger Hunt is the first forward I put in.

'He was such a reliable scorer that he gave his side a chance in every game, no matter what the odds. He always provided an outlet when we were under the cosh. He had wonderful ball control and could hold it up brilliantly. He carried the ball two feet in front of him and defenders had trouble tackling him because of his control.

'Roger's a great lad, too, smashing to have a pint with. He's an unassuming, level-headed fellow, never the slightest bit bombastic despite all his achievements.

'He's still adored on Merseyside, but at Anfield in the old days there was always someone who differed, whatever the subject. There was one fellow who would write to Roger every Monday morning and no matter what the result had been or what Roger's performance had been like, the letter would be addressed to "Over-The-Bar Hunt".

'He thought Roger was the worst player in the world, but Roger would just laugh at it and pass it around so we could all enjoy it.

'Before 1960 Liverpool were known as "Liddellpool", essentially an average team with one marvellous player. Roger became one of a number of outstanding players in a wonderful side. In many ways he was THE new symbol of the club's burning desire to succeed under Bill Shankly.'

IAN CALLAGHAN of Liverpool and England

'Roger made his debut just ahead of me, but we grew up together in the Liverpool side and spent the 1960s as a right-wing partnership. He'll tell you that he gave me my first pass - and I'll tell you that it was a bad one!

'Having cleared that up, I must add that I was in the perfect position to see most of his performances at close quarters, and that was a privilege.

'Roger was great to play alongside because he didn't wait for you to do his work for him. He was always there as an option, having made the effort to find space, often with defenders on his back. He was very strong and a tremendous athlete with broad shoulders and muscular legs, a bit like Mark Hughes in that respect.

'Of course, because he never stopped running he tended to be described as just a workhorse, but that was not the case. He was a wonderful poacher of goals and an excellent all-round footballer.

'Roger didn't have an aggressive nature, either on or off the field. When he was fouled - and he had to put up with plenty of that - he never retaliated, just wiped himself down and got on with the game. That attitude made him a tremendous favourite.

'He was always a quiet guy, but one who spoke up when necessary and his team-mates had immense respect for him. He's a totally genuine lad, too. Once he's a friend he's a friend for life.

'Yet everything he does, he does to win, right down to a friendly game of golf. He always plays fair but he gives everything and concentrates fiercely. That's part of his make-up and it played a tremendous part in his football success.'

BOBBY CHARLTON of Manchester United and England

'I was always glad to see Roger Hunt beside me in the England team. Personal glory was never his thing, but although he never felt the need to blow his own trumpet, he was a strong personality in his own right. Certainly, he was hugely missed if he wasn't there. He took the load for lots of people - I know he did an awful lot for me.

'Any team needs to do things together and he was a great team man. You could make plans around him; he was loyal, determined and utterly dependable. If Roger said he would do something, then he would do it, no question about it.

'He was tough physically and totally unselfish, running off the ball to make things happen for others. But he had plenty of talent, too; he was pretty well two-footed and if the 'keeper dropped the ball then Roger had a knack of tucking away the half-chance.

'He contributed a great deal to Liverpool's success, far more than just his goals. When they lost the ball they always won it back as quickly as possible, and much of that was down to Roger. He would chase and harry, all across the front line. As soon as you had the ball, that team of Bill Shankly's would crowd you, never giving you time to think.

'If you wanted to beat Liverpool you knew you'd have to work as hard as them. That meant working as hard as Roger Hunt - and that wasn't easy.

'Jimmy Greaves probably had a better touch, but Roger had so many other attributes. People said Jimmy was the easier of the two to look at, and they were probably right. He was more graceful, what we used to call a southern type of footballer. Roger was more of the northern type - and none the worse for that!

'Roger was, and still is, an absolute gentleman and a quiet lad who never shouted the odds, but he had a lovely sense of humour.

'I remember one occasion when we were both in Spain with the Variety Club of Great Britain and had played golf all week. Roger had to leave on the Thursday because of his commitments with the Pools Panel and he asked me if I needed a caddy. He said he was sorry for the lad who had been caddying for him, who was upset by Roger's enforced early departure, and he recommended him thoroughly.

'As it happened I did need someone, and I took this lad of Roger's. The next day at the first hole, he gave me some very strange advice, telling me to use a four-iron when I was 350 yards from the green. I thought I'd better bow to his local knowledge and expertise but it didn't exactly work out. Then we reached the green, which had a massive slope, but he told me to play only six inches to the right - I did, and I missed by a mile.

'This sort of thing went on all day and it turned out Roger had stitched me up wickedly. He'd found the worst caddy he'd ever known and he thought he'd pass him on to me. I'm still looking to get my own back!'

PHIL THOMPSON of Liverpool and England

'I went to a function the other night and he was on the top table - and people were still calling him Sir Roger. It's something that's stuck not only because of his achievements, but also through his personality. To the people who know him, and to the fans, it seems fitting, somehow.

'As the main goal-scorer, he was the hero to a whole generation. I always remember joining Liverpool and not quite believing that I was there alongside Roger Hunt.

'I was only 15 and he was a star. I'd see him in the dressing-room when I sneaked in to take kit to the drying-room, one of the apprentices' many chores.

'I used to look at him in awe. I used to be amazed that I could be close to him and that he was calling me Phil. Shanks was the father figure but Roger Hunt was something special. It might sound daft, but just picking up his sweaty kit gave me satisfaction.

'He was very polite, great with all the youngsters. Some top players would treat you as a lackey, fetching and carrying, but not Roger. You could talk to him, he was always approachable, always had time for you. He never humiliated you with a snappy reply. That's so important to impressionable apprentices.

'I trained with him in pre-season 1969/70 and it was a privilege. I was so overawed I'd be embarrassed. Even if I'd been released after two years, in some ways I'd have left fulfilled - just being able to tell my mates I'd trained with Roger Hunt. I'm proud to have known him. His greatness will never dim on Merseyside.

'I couldn't believe it when there was criticism from the Kop when the goals began to dry up late in his career. I stood there and people all around me were slagging him. But when a replacement missed a chance it was all "Roger would have scored that!" Me, I never doubted that he was the greatest.

'When that great Liverpool team broke up and he went to Bolton, I always used to look for their result. People were going up there from Liverpool, just to watch Roger play, and sometimes that was when Liverpool were at home. They added a few hundred to the Burnden Park gate - all because they wanted to watch The Man.'

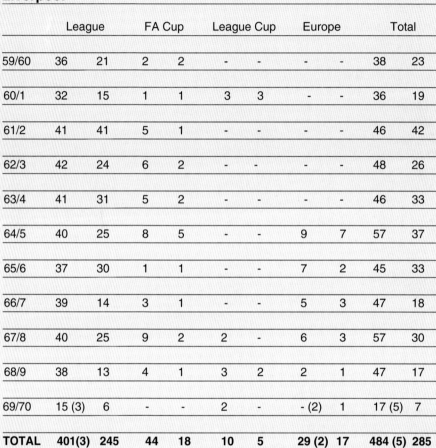

Liverpool

	League		FA Cup		League Cup		Europe		Total	
59/60	36	21	2	2	-	-	-	-	38	23
60/1	32	15	1	1	3	3	-	-	36	19
61/2	41	41	5	1	-	-	-	-	46	42
62/3	42	24	6	2	-	-	-	-	48	26
63/4	41	31	5	2	-	-	-	-	46	33
64/5	40	25	8	5	-	-	9	7	57	37
65/6	37	30	1	1	-	-	7	2	45	33
66/7	39	14	3	1	-	-	5	3	47	18
67/8	40	25	9	2	2	-	6	3	57	30
68/9	38	13	4	1	3	2	2	1	47	17
69/70	15 (3)	6	-	-	2	-	- (2)	1	17 (5)	7
TOTAL	**401(3)**	**245**	**44**	**18**	**10**	**5**	**29 (2)**	**17**	**484 (5)**	**285**

Bolton Wanderers

	League		FA Cup		League Cup		Europe		Total	
69/70	17	5	1	0	-	-	-	-	18	5
70/1	22 (2)	8	-	-	1 (1)	-	-	-	23 (3)	8
71/2	33 (2)	11	1 (1)	1	2 (1)	-	-	-	36 (4)	12
TOTAL	**72 (4)**	**24**	**2 (1)**	**1**	**3 (2)**	**0**	**-**	**-**	**77(7)**	**25**

England

Date	Opponents	Venue	Result		Hunt goals
2.4.62	Austria	Wembley	Won	3-1	1
2.6.63	East Germany	Leipzig	Won	2-1	1
11.4.64	Scotland	Hampden Park	Lost	0-1	-
27.5.64	USA	New York	Won	10-0	4
4.6.64	Portugal	Sao Paulo	Drew	1-1	1
18.11.64	Wales	Wembley	Won	2-1	-
8.12.65	Spain	Bernabeu	Won	2-0	1
5.1.66	Poland	Goodison Park	Drew	1-1	-
23.2.66	West Germany	Wembley	Won	1-0	-
2.4.66	Scotland	Hampden Park	Won	4-3	2
26.6.66	Finland	Helsinki	Won	3-0	1
29.6.66	Norway	Oslo	Won	6-1	-
5.7.66	Poland	Chorzow	Won	1-0	1
11.7.66	Uruguay	Wembley	Drew	0-0	-
16.7.66	Mexico	Wembley	Won	2-0	1
20.7.66	France	Wembley	Won	2-0	2
23.7.66	Argentina	Wembley	Won	1-0	-
26.7.66	Portugal	Wembley	Won	2-1	-
30.7.66	West Germany	Wembley	Won	4-2	-
22.10.66	N Ireland	Windsor Park	Won	2-0	1
2.11.66	Czechoslovakia	Wembley	Drew	0-0	-
16.11.66	Wales	Wembley	Won	5-1	-
24.5.67	Spain	Wembley	Won	2-0	1
27.5.67	Austria	Vienna	Won	1-0	-
21.10.67	Wales	Ninian Park	Won	3-0	-
22.11.67	N Ireland	Wembley	Won	2-0	-
6.12.67	USSR	Wembley	Drew	2-2	-
3.4.68	Spain	Wembley	Won	1-0	-
8.5.68	Spain	Bernabeu	Won	2-1	-
22.5.68	Sweden	Wembley	Won	3-1	1
5.6.68	Yugoslavia	Florence	Lost	0-1	-
8.6.68	USSR	Rome	Won	2-0	-
6.11.68	Rumania	Bucharest	Drew	0-0	-
15.1.69	Rumania	Wembley	Drew	1-1	-

Roger won 34 caps and scored 18 goals.

Football League

Date	Opponents	Venue	Result		Hunt goals
21.3.62	Scottish League	Villa Park	Lost	3-4	2
2.10.63	League of Ireland	Dublin	Lost	1-2	-
9.5.64	Italian League	Milan	Lost	0-1	-
28.10.64	Irish League	Belfast	Won	4-0	-
20.3.68	Scottish League	Ayresome Park	Won	2-0	1

Roger made five Inter-League appearances and scored three goals.

The benchmark by which all Liverpool strikers are judged. Roger holds the Red's record of 245 League strikes, which Ian Rush was chasing in 1995/96. As the season started he was 21 adrift; at 33 and with Robbie Fowler and Stan Collymore in contention for places, time was not on his side.

BIBLIOGRAPHY

The Boot Room by Ivan Ponting and Steve Hale, Bluecoat Press, 1994

Liverpool In Europe by Steve Hale and Ivan Ponting, Guinness Publishing, 1992

Liverpool FC: Season 1959/60, edited by Eddie Marks, Marksport, 1986

Liverpool Player By Player by Ivan Ponting, Crowood Press, 1990

Hunt For Goals by Roger Hunt with David Prole, Pelham Books, 1969

Liverpool: A Complete Record by Brian Pead, Breedon Books, 1988

Shankly by Bill Shankly, Arthur Barker, 1976

Shankly by Phil Thompson, Bluecoat Press, 1993

The FA Cup Final - A Post-War History by Ivan Ponting, TW Publications, 1993

England: The Complete Post-War Record by Mike Payne, Breedon Books, 1993

World Cup '66 by Hugh McIlvanney, Eyre and Spottiswoode, 1966

Football League Players Records 1946-92 by Barry Hugman, TW Publications, 1992